Finding the Way to Life's Purpose

Will give you a better understanding and
a different outlook to Life's Purpose

****

Can be used as a Reference Guide

****

Will give a different look of
what this thing called life is all about

Gilbert Rudy Castillo

Writers' Branding
1800-608-6550
www.writersbranding.com
orders@writersbranding.com

CONTENTS

DEDICATION

To my first wife, who acted in pure faith on a vision that was given to her, as she knelt at the altar to pray to her Maker. Since then, she had the privilege of going to meet Him . She was able to see this vision with her eyes open. She could see a cottage with a sign over it, and it read GUATEMALA.

At that time, she did not know what it meant. As she started to inquire about, she found out that the word was the name of a country located in Central America. At that time, once she understood the vision, she started to make plans to go to Guatemala to be a missionary for Christ.

She and another family went there to start a new mission and got situated in a village next to mine. Not too far from my home. It was at that mission I decided to go and talk to the missionary, as I was shopping for a Church to belong to. It was at this mission I gave my life to Christ and became a Christian.

It also was there where we met, and we got married. Being a farmer, I could not give full time to help the mission. As the time of planting and harvesting came, I had to leave the mission in order to attend to my crops.

After a year of helping the mission, the missionary suggested that both of us should go to the States and make some money to pay hire hands at my farm so I could give full time to the mission. We came to the States and became our home, until she passed away and remains my home, till this day.

CHAPTER ONE

PHASE ONE

First, let's talk a little about this thing called life and the humans that possess it. I will mention some things that you already know or some time in your life you might have heard. After refreshing our minds about life, it is very likely that it will take us to a place and position of awareness of ourselves. It will reveal who we really are and where we are going, but most important, it will show us how we can get there.

Life is that thing that brings us into existence, in conjunction with the physical body. It is what makes us alive and the person we are. It is what other people see in us as a human being, but also, as what we see in the mirror, a unique individual capable of existing among others in this world. But we are sent and placed on this world to play a part as intelligent human beings, who are capable of deciphering many things on our own, possessing many special qualities and talents not yet discovered.

Somehow, without any alternative or choice of our own, life begins in us, and it will take us somewhere without having to make any decisions of our own if we just choose to do so. It will continue until we are deceased or get cut off from this world we call home.

The good thing is that we have and possess the ability to determine where the end of our life's journey can take us or where we will end up. It will be based on the decisions and choices we make. Keeping in mind that if you do not make any choices, life does not come to a standstill. It will take you most likely to a place or places not to your liking. Most of the time, it is influenced by others or our surroundings. But for some people, it will be late to make any corrections. The reason being is that we do not know what the future have for us, yet we can and have the ability to change it and take the right direction if we choose to do so.

There are times when people will drive themselves to the place of no return, and it will be late to make any corrections to the style of life you are in.

I would say why wait till then to start and make the changes now while you can. Or as a result of your doings, you can end up either in jail for life or make yourself sick with a terminal disease or end up dead. Therefore cheating yourselves of a profitable, successful, joyful, and wonderful life you could have chosen.

Now, let's talk about us. One of the things most people struggle with is this question: How we came to Earth in the first place, and as you know, we did not have any say on it and for most have on-answered questions about themselves. There is a theory out there about a big bang that happened millions of years ago. And as a result of it, everything we see, touch, and smell came into existence including mankind. We also have been told that we are animals of special breed, but none of this is true! We are individuals, one of a kind, humans that were placed here with a purpose.

We were sent to this world, and we are here not because we chose to. Let's say that now that we are here, have you ever thought of what the house, apartment, or condo where you live would be like if you were not there? Or what your neighborhood would be like without you? One step further is: What would your family be like without you? Would there be a family without you?

It is hard to understand or imagine it, but it takes all of us to make what we call families, neighborhoods, towns, cities, countries, or should we say, it takes all of us to make what we know as our world. In any case, we as individuals play an important part in making up our society. In one way or another, for most of us, we do contribute, even if it is on a small scale. Yet we still feel lost and sometimes out of place.

We as humans have special qualities and abilities. Most of us have talents that will remain undiscovered. Because, many times, it takes another individual to bring it out of us and discover that hidden talent. In many of those cases, we can attribute it to our parents or our teachers. Also, a stranger in our life can help to bring it out of us as well. At one time or another, we will play an important role in someone's life. Without you, some of those talents will never come to pass. You could be one of those parties I mentioned above: You could be the parent, teacher, or one of the strangers.

Talking about having to play a role on someone's life! There are some people that have very little regard for the same (life), so little that they will not even hesitate to think and make sure that you or whosoever stands on their way will be terminated. They will take away your life and make sure that you cease to exist without any regard for life whatsoever.

The point is, what about those who are cut off short? Could it be one of them who was to help you in discovering your talent? Not only that, but this person was robbed of their role in life and also has affected others as well. That has created another problem, not only for the deceased, but also to the one who took that life away, and that is, that in most cases the one who stopped to exist will no longer have the chance to make things right or have any time to fix unresolved items with others. People on either case have neglected to find the real reason for which they exist and therefore giving room to lose many things, principally the respect for life itself and interfering with the existence of others. If you do, maybe that would tell you that you do not or should not interfere with(the reason for their existence) and go as far as taking their life away from them and disrupt a series of events and keep them from doing what only they could do.

As I mentioned above, we have been told that some time back there was a big bang, and that all we know, see, and touch came from it, but if you look around you, you know that this theory is not supported by any stretch of the imagination. It took a superior being with intelligence, imagination, and perhaps we can safely say with some humor as well, but most of all it took an excellent taste for color and beauty to accomplish what we know, see, touch, hear, and smell.

If we can see and understand that, then we know that it had to be that person or being that brought it all into existence. Then it is much easier to see that was Him, who also brought us into existence, as the good Book tells us and gives us a description on how it all took place. Not only He gave us the privilege to exist, but He also gave us many qualities that can only be found on humans as part of the uniqueness that we possess and many times we exercised. We have found that animals also possess a better characteristic not found in humans, such as hearing. Some animals can hear things that we cannot hear or smell, and in other cases, sense of direction, for example: a turtle can find water after it surfaces from the nest. Penguins can also find water when they are even miles from it. Watching a movie once, I observe that a calf had been stolen and was put into a herd of many others. Then the owner of the calf found himself with an impossible task.

It was quickly resolved when he thought to bring the mother of the calf and walked it around the herd to find her spring.

That was a sense of recognition found only on animals. I also have heard about babies getting switched in the hospital from their mother, and the sad part is that the mother never notes it.

Talking about special qualities, it is up to us to develop the character we possess, and it is adjustable and also adaptable, based on the part of the world that we are born in at, and it will influence the language we will speak and the environment that we will grow up in. It will determine the type of behavior that we will develop in ourselves, and it will be based on the influence of our surroundings. As we know, many things were passed on by our ancestors to us, therefore, it depends on the examples we get and pass down to our offspring, both the good and bad habits. Many of which we blame on our surroundings and sometimes we blame our ancestors.

The minute we come into this world, we are something special, no two are alike, even though in this age, our scientists are working on cloning humans; it will not work based on what we read in the good book (the Bible). There are no two spirits or souls that are the same; we are created individuals for God's purpose. Included in all of these, there is a special item! That is, the ability to make choices of our own, and perhaps in some cases, we can get out or come out of some habits or customs we find ourselves in. It can be from either bad or good as a result of our decision. God has not left us alone to defend for ourselves; He has provided for us some guidelines for us to follow if we choose to do so. But if we decide to go contrary to His guidelines, then the chance of finding ourselves tangle up in some of the things described above is greater. We find some of them in the New Testament the Book of *Romans 13:8 Owe no man any thing, but to love one another: for he that loveth another hath fulfilled the law. :9 For this, Thou shalt not commit adultery, Thou shalt not kill, Thou shalt not steal, Thou shalt not bear false witness, Thou shalt not covet; and if [there be] any other commandment, it is briefly comprehended in this saying, namely, Thou shalt love thy neighbor as thyself.*

Can you imagine how our world would be if everybody would obey those commandments? It would be like what God intended it to be.

For now, or for just a moment, let's forget the idea of being a religious person or even a Christian. *If* you apply those rules to yourself, you will find out that it would have a tremendous impact on your life for the good. You will find out also, that most countries have adopted the same rules to govern themselves with. As of today, they are all based on the Bible, or God's way of government, which in turn is God's way to begin with.

Why the need for rules, you might ask? And the answer is this: When you get a group of people together, they will form what we know as a community, town, or as much as a city, and start to communicate with each other, interacting in business and pleasure. They will have a variety of transactions with each other, which in time will bring out the human nature out of them, for some, it is more obvious than others to become that bad person. In all cases, they have to adopt some rules in order to respect the boundaries of others and keep piece among themselves or things will start to go out of control. That is how we humans have become with the need of rules or laws and elected some of them to apply the laws to the people.

As a result of all of this, problems will arise when someone will fail to respect the boundaries of others, and some are or will become unruly as part of the old nature we are born with (more on this later).

That is what drives people and give them the impulse to do wrong and wants to be free of any laws or regulations. Wanting nothing, but to satisfy oneself, whatever it might be. But for most, they will be looking for a leader or someone to bring their problems to and decipher them to us.

Someone that has been given the power to enforce the rules, usually adapted as a result of a group or town meetings. Where they are elected and given the authority to enforce the law and to control the uncontrollable. And have some order in their neighborhood and society in general. It has gotten to the place where is necessary to have different methods of punishments. All because of what some people's interpretation of freedom is. Or what they think of what being free is all about, or the interpretation of what they think they deserve.

In a conversation with this coworker I had at one of my Jobs, he brought up what his idea of being free was or his perception of freedom. What he wanted to do was not heaving to answer to anyone just to do whatever pleased him, without any intervention from anybody else. His idea was to get up whenever he wanted, go anywhere he wanted, go to work whenever he wanted, and go home whenever he wanted as well. Even though it sounded good, it was a big surprise for me. I never heard anyone express themselves that way before. Then I gave him an example by saying, that not even the owner/employer that we work for was able to do that. He has a responsibility to the company and to us the employees. I continue to tell him, you need to understand that all has a price, including freedom. You can't be yourself when there are others around you or you will interfere with theirs. You have to respect their freedom as well, which is limited to all. Take for instance our job! We agree to get paid in exchange for our labor, therefore, we have a duty to perform, and the rules are made by the employer, in this case within the laws of the State where we are. We agree to come in at 8:00 in the morning, have a lunch at 12:00 noon, off at 5:00 p.m., and a ten-minute break in between each of the four hours that we work. You cannot come to work any time you want or whenever you want, or live any time you want! Unless there is a legal agreement between you and your employer, or he can dismiss you (have you fired)! You will lose your job as simple as that, or he can refuse to pay you for not completing your work of eight hours a day. Especially today employers are very careful when it comes to hiring someone; they want reliable and dependable workers. Whatever you do, you cannot step on someone else's toes, as the saying goes; you will have to pay for the consequences thereof, and in this case, you may even end up paying a fine or end up going to jail. Even freedom has its price.

That conversation I never forgot. I did not imagine that there is any one with this kind of mentality, especially in a city as big as this one, where we were at that time, where there are all kinds of interactions between people of different lands and cultures, and even different languages as well. That co-worker, I gave him lots of things to think about. The one thing we need to remember is: We were put here on this place, wherever that might be in this world of ours, and this is our Creator's world according to the Old Testament, the book of *Psalms 24:1: The earth [is] the LORD'S, and the fullness thereof; the world, and they that dwell therein.*

Everything is His, and for some reason, humanity has forgotten it, or maybe we can safely say that we have failed to pass it down through the generations or have chosen to ignore it all together. As a result of it, we have been getting farther and farther apart from Him. He always wanted to take care of us if we just let Him and give Him the chance. We read in the book of *Mt 23:37: O Jerusalem, Jerusalem, thou that killest the prophets, and stonest them which are sent unto thee, how often would I have gathered thy children together, even as a hen gathereth her chickens under her wings, and ye would not!*

But it has been much easier to ignore Him. Maybe if we let Him, we would not be tangle up in the problems we find ourselves in. Surprisingly people will blame others for their mistakes, even to the point that they will blame God as well, and it is hard to admit that we are wrong, it is much easier to say that someone else did it and pass the blame to others, even when we know it might cost their reputation, or even their life.

As a rule, people don't like to admit guilt for the fear of punishment. There have been times when I asked someone what they think about themselves! Have you ever thought or consider yourself to be a bad person or a sinner? The answer is no! I don't consider myself to be bad or sinner. Most people like to think that they are good people and maybe they are, or that is what they like to think or believe of themselves.

It has been a big problem that gets in the way when you try to share to them the Gospel and accept Christ into their life (meaning, you have to admit that you're a sinner), being that the primary reason that they don't need Him. If you think you are not a sinner and you consider yourself to be a good person, why would you need Christ for anyway? And they would be right!

In some cases when you look around, everything is going fine, you have a good job or business, you have everything you want and work for, perhaps you have a better house than the average person, and as far as you know, even your health is good, so what would you need Christ for?

If it wasn't because the Scriptures tells us that the whole human race has been lost, almost from the beginning of our existence, we would never have known it. Furthermore, we choose to ignore it, to the place that most people do not even know, that we have been lost. Jesus confirmed it when He said that He came to save the sinner and the lost. *Matthew 18:11: For the Son of man is come to save that which was lost. 17: When Jesus heard it, he saith unto them, They that are whole have no need of the physician, but they that are sick: I came not to call the righteous, but sinners to repentance.*

The sad part in all of this is, that The Bible tells us that we all are sinners. *Romans 5:12: Wherefore, as by one man sin entered into the world, and death by sin; and so death passed upon all men, for that all have sinned:*

I found myself in that category when I was in my teenage years. For different reasons, I did not smoke, drink, and even manage to stay away from foul language, so I consider myself to be a pretty good guy. It took a different kind of convincing from the Lord to get through to me! And He had to bring me to a place where I could find my own conviction and come to the conclusion that I needed Christ in my life, but also the need to be forgiven of my sins.

Christ uses different methods with different people to get through to them, depending on the circumstances we find ourselves in. Some will come right out and admit that they are sinners, but a lot of us do not. For me to come out and say or admit that I was a sinner, it took a little different twist, a different way to be convinced and accept that I was a sinner.

It all got started when I saw a friend of mine with a little tiny book I had never seen before; it was a New Testament. I asked him to sell it to me, and he accepted! At that time things were a lot less expensive than now, and I bought it from him for 25 cents. But it was also a day labor price at that time.

Then I started to read it and read it from cover to cover. My first thought when I started to read it was that it sounded like it might be a USA tactic to overtake a country like mine (being a Central American). At that time, the only people I knew that had bibles were the missionaries that came from United States. But the more I read it, the more I came to see that the main character was Christ! And I was able to see that He was a Jew from the land of Israel. I began to see that all of the stories in this book originated in Israel, so it could not have been a USA tactic.

But guess what! It took a more drastic measure to convince Paul than me, when he was confronted by Christ on the way to Damascus. (Being Paul the writer of most of the New Testament books.) He shook him down off his horse and he was blind for several days. We read his story in *Acts 9:3: And as he journeyed, he came near Damascus: and suddenly there shined round about him a light from heaven: :4 And he fell to the earth, and heard a voice saying unto him, Saul, Saul, why persecutest thou me? :5 And he said, Who art thou, Lord? And the Lord said, I am Jesus whom thou persecutest: [it is] hard for thee to kick against the pricks.*

Up to this time, Paul had been persecuting the Christians of his time. Even after this, he could still have refused to yield to God's calling and miss it all. We would not have all of the books he wrote if he had rejected the call.

I'm grateful to the Lord for being so faithful in calling me! He gave me the privilege of being able to obey his calling. Not only that, but I was also able to make a decision to go all the way or nothing, and I was able to see that it was worth more than I could ever imagine.

Now I like for you to consider this: Do not wait for God to shake you, it might never happen. But you need to remain aware of His calling when it comes. *Rv 3:20: Behold, I stand at the door, and knock: if any man hear my voice, and open the door, I will come in to him, and will sup with him, and he with me.* And I hope you will take the right steps to accept and follow Him.

The same thing happened, or similar to mine, to a coworker, when he found out that I was a Christian. The first question he gave me was when he said, "Why are you practicing white people's religion?" I was so stunned when I heard him say that because I went through a similar way of thinking myself when I started to read the New Testament. For me, to answer that question was a little easier because I had similar thoughts myself. I proceeded by asking him a question: "Where did you get the idea that Christianity is white people's religion?" I went on to say and explain to him that Christ is of Jewish descent and that's all what the Bible talks about; it happened in the area of Israel and not here in the USA. (When you read the Bible, you will find out that God picked a young lady of Jewish descent to have Christ born by into this world.) His mouth seemed like it dropped down, and after that, he had no more questions or things to say. But my biggest surprise was when I discovered that the Bible is the best history book we have, even as of today. And all the places that it talks about, they really exist, and some of them you can actually go and see them for yourself today. They are now referred to as places and things of the Holy Land.

My suggestion to you is that you need to read it at least once in your lifetime, and at least the New Testament. You will, like me, no longer see life the same way, as I saw it before I read that little book. It brought a totally different point of view into my own way of thinking. It is a book of facts. But best of all, it is a road map of where you can go. It will show you and continue to do lots of good for the rest of your life. Especially when you know where you are going and where you will end up and where you will spend eternity.

When you read through the Bible, you will see how God has created our universe, our world, and all the things in it, then He created men, and out of men, He created women to be the men's companion.

(You can read this in the first book of the Bible or Old Testament.) Also you will see the fall of men from the grace of God. But in order for God to restore what was His original intent after men fell, he already had a plan that included sending His only Son to die for all mankind. But all of that came with some guidelines for us to follow and how to go about fulfilling His requirements. The catch is to do it His way, and not ours (as many like to do). You cannot become a Christian or a follower of Christ on your own terms; it has to be on His only. We need to realize that He already set the rules, and they are there for us to follow. Surprisingly there are too many people that want to become Christians on their own terms, and not His. That does not work, and you will accomplish nothing. We read that there is a group of people that came there surprised when they found out that they had missed the coming of the bridegroom. *Mat. 25:11: Afterward came also the other virgins, saying, Lord, Lord, open to us. 12: But he answered and said, Verily I say unto you, I know you not.*

(Referring to Christ) And the Lord said to them, "I never knew you." *Mat. 7:22: Many will say to me in that day, Lord, Lord, have we not prophesied in thy name? and in thy name have cast out devils? and in thy name done many wonderful works?*
23: And then will I profess unto them, I never knew you: depart from me, ye that work iniquity.

And He responded the same way to both groups. Obviously, we need to be aware of not falling in the same category ourselves.

The Bible tells us that the way to destruction is wider, and many are the ones who find it. *Mat. 7:13 Enter ye in at the strait gate: for wide is the gate, and broad is the way, that leadeth to destruction, and many there be which go in thereat,*

I am very sure that I do not want to be one of those people. My prayers and my desire are that you should not be one of them either.

As you read the Bible, you will find out that the consequences of sin is death. Because of that, He does not want us to perish, but that we might have everlasting life. *Romans 6:23: For the wages of sin is death; but the gift of God is eternal life through Jesus Christ our Lord.*

Even though most of us consider this thing called life to be a precious possession we have and cherish it and like to extend it for as long as we can. Plus, we try to enjoy it to the extent as possible, yet when we are offered not only a better quality of it and extend it to eternity, we seem to refuse to accept it. The logical thinking is that we do want it, but only on our own terms and we fail to see that sin has disturbed the logic in our way of thinking.

But before we go any farther, we need to define what SIN is based or according to what God and the Bible describes it to be.

Also we find that the scriptures make a distinction between the one that Adam and Eve made, which we inherit and are born with. But there is also the one we commit. Keeping in mind that there are two (2) types of sin mentioned in the Bible, and God duly treat each one differently.

1) The first is referred to as the **original** sin, or Adam and Eve's; and
2) The second is **sin of omission**; or the one "we" commit ourselves. Very important to keep the two separate because they are treated and are taken care of on a separate and different way. For the simple reason that we are not capable of repenting from the original sin. But it is detectable by oneself by the fruit that it produces.

The **original sin** came to be when Adam was given a specific instruction order (commandment) to follow. *Gen. 2:16: And the LORD God commanded the man, saying, Of every tree of the garden thou mayest freely eat: 17: But of the tree of the knowledge of good and evil, thou shalt not eat of it: for in the day that thou eatest thereof thou shalt surely die.*

What happened in this passage is that Adam simply did not keep and obey the commandment that was given to Him, so he was disobedient to God's commandment. As a result of the disobedience, he was told that at the day he would eat of the tree, he would die, and he did, not as we know death of the body but spiritual death. In other words, he broke the spiritual relationship that he had between him and

God, and as part of this disobedience, there were other things added to the consequences, being one of them hard labor. And since we were made of dust, to dust we will return when we die in our physical body. *Gen. 3:17: And unto Adam he said, Because thou hast hearkened unto the voice of thy wife, and hast eaten of the tree, of which I commanded thee, saying, Thou shalt not eat of it: cursed is the ground for thy sake; in sorrow shalt thou eat of it all the days of thy life; 18: Thorns also and thistles shall it bring forth to thee; and thou shalt eat the herb of the field; 19: In the sweat of thy face shalt thou eat bread, till thou return unto the ground; for out of it wast thou taken: for dust thou art, and unto dust shalt thou return.*

To the woman, God gave her a punishment as well. *Gen. 6:16: Unto the woman he said, I will greatly multiply thy sorrow and thy conception; in sorrow thou shalt bring forth children; and thy desire shall be to thy husband, and he shall rule over thee.*

To the serpent that initiated this whole ordeal, on the verses before, it was given a punishment as well. *Gen. 3:14: And the LORD God said unto the serpent, Because thou hast done this, thou art cursed above all cattle, and above every beast of the field; upon thy belly shalt thou go, and dust shalt thou eat all the days of thy life:*
15: And I will put enmity between thee and the woman, and between thy seed and her seed; it shall bruise thy head, and thou shalt bruise his heel.

It is hard to understand that a simple disobedience can make so much damage like this one. This is the one that put the entire human race in the mess we find it even to today. It will continue for as long there are people being born and living on this world. But this is not all! If you can see that this is the sin that we inherited when we are born, or should we say that we are born in sin, because of the sin of disobedience that originated in Adam, our first father. From this sin is where we get our impulses from within that drive us to do the wrong things or where we get the impulse to sin! And as long as the original sin is in us, it will drive us to sin and will continue to do so for as long as it remains there. We can thank God for providing us with a way out of it. He has provided a way to get rid of it (the original sin) out of us. (More on this later.)

The second is referred to as the **sin of omission**. Christ referred to it when He gave the reason for us to be forgiven. *Mat. 6:14 For if ye forgive men their trespasses, your heavenly Father will also forgive you:* and in *John 5:14: Afterward Jesus findeth him in the temple, and said unto him, Behold, thou art made whole: sin no more, lest a worse thing come unto thee.*

Jesus told this man to stop sinning, and John the Baptist preached the baptism of repentance for the forgiveness of sin. In this case, it is the repentance for the sin of omission (the sin we commit). *Mark 1:4: John did baptize in the wilderness, and preach the baptism of repentance for the remission of sins.*

Talking in the plural or meaning that we do commit more than one sin, while Adam's sin is referred to in the singular.

This is the sin that we commit and all mankind needs to repent from. It is one of those things that you can't ignore or leave unresolved. The sad part is that most people do not do anything about it, and lacking the knowledge of it, we will never know that sin will dictate the direction you will take in life. It will determine not only the type or kind of life you will continue to live, but also at the end of all, it will determine where you end up. When you cease to existence or come to the end of your journey on earth, you will either go to heaven or to the lake of fire as the Bible describes it when you read the last book of the New Testament. *Rv 20:15: And whosoever was not found written in the book of life was cast into the lake of fire.*

Now God's original intent or plan is to have us in His presence for eternity. And still is. He has provided a way for us to turn from where we are to His original plan. He also gave us a special ingredient or ability, and that is to be able to make a choice of our own to either choose and follow Him as our God and savior, or not. Under no circumstances are we obligated to become His servants or be converted to Christianity. For those who decide to follow God's way, He has given them the privilege that for all eternity will be with Him in glory. To those who do not, they are sent to be with the devil and his fallen angels into the lake of fire prepared just for them. *Mat. 25:41: Then shall he say also unto them on the left hand, Depart from me, ye cursed, into everlasting fire, prepared for the devil and his angels.*

As the saying goes, He laid it all for us to follow, and now it is up to us to pick which way we want to go. The best thing of all of this is that we still have the option to change it later if we choose to do so. That will only happen if we are able to recognize that we made the wrong decision when we went the wrong way. And we realized that we are going in the opposite direction and we continue to go the wrong way. And continue to live in sin.

If you can do that, then you can turn to Christ. Sadly for some, they will never know, as they continue to ignore all the warnings, or Christ's call that comes to them.

Another way of thinking is that you might say, I am going to do all I can to have fun, or I'm too young, and when I'm old and tired of it, then I will turn from sin, and I will go and serve Christ, and I will become a Christian. The problem with this theory is that there are things we don't know, and we don't have any control over them. If we decide to take this approach, we need to fully understand that is our life we are dealing with.

And I know that there are some that don't care much about it. The problem is that we do not know, or have any control over what the future will bring to us, and how much time we have left of our life. We are very limited when it comes to knowing or predicting the future.

Another bad news is: Because we do not have any control over the future, death can call us at any time. No one knows when we are going to die, and we may end up missing everything, especially the opportunity to take care of unfinished and unresolved business, or many other things when we think that we have all the time in the world to do as we please. *Mat. 25:13: Watch therefore, for ye know neither the day nor the hour wherein the Son of man cometh.*

This passage shows us that we need to be ready and prepared for His coming, at all times, without wasting any time; and for some will be sooner than later. *Hebrews 9:27: And as it is appointed unto men once to die, but after this the judgment.*

That shows that not everything ends when we die. The theory of ending all when we die, this passage disproves it.

We will be brought to justice after we die or cross to the other side. That means that life continues after death, and now we must prepare ourselves today, not tomorrow, to cross that final line. This puts us in a position of having to correct the problems as soon as we can or when they are pointed to you, and come to realize that you are a sinner, and in need of Christ.

Up to this time, we can see that God has done everything in His own power to restore what has been lost. To describe it from a different point of view, I will give you an illustration I heard when I first started to attend Church, in one of the re-bibles that I attended. It is a story about the railroad as it made its way to the Old West.

This railroad engineer was tracing the route in which to lay the rails. While scouting the land, he came across this hill that it stood on the way. It needed to be removed in order to keep the rails as level as much it was possible. When he got to the hill, he happened to notice that in the middle of it, there was a very large colony of ants. So he stopped to observe them, and he saw how big the ant colony was and how busy all the ants were. Then he thought to himself, if there was anything that he could do for those ants, to make them move to another location, in order to save their lives. After observing them for a while, the only thing he came up with was this: If he could become an ant and go down there, and tell them of the danger that is coming to them if they remain in this place. Then he thought to himself, even if he could do that, he will be like them, not knowing of the danger that approaches, and all of them would be lost and his endeavor would be for nothing. So he said to himself, the only way would be for him to become an ant, but be able to retain all his human abilities, and be able to go and tell them of what is coming and to convince them to move to another location to avoid all that tragedy and loss of lives. But also to have the ability to return to where I got started from; being a human and see that his plan has been carried out successfully. Then go and give the order to send all the equipment to cut and level the hill and make way for the railroad. But at this time knowing that the ants are saved at their new location.

That is exactly what Christ has done for us, when he came to this earth to warn us of the lake of fire and the eternal damnation that was designed for the devil and his angels. This is the reason why Christ came to die and shed his blood for us. Except that the difference between Christ and the engineer is Love. He loves us so much that not only wants to save us, but he also wants us to partake of eternal life with Him. *John 3:17: For God sent not his Son into the world to condemn the world; but that the world through him might be saved. Mark 14:24 And he said unto them, This is my blood of the new testament, which is shed for many. Mathew 26:28 For this is my blood of the new testament, which is shed for many for the remission of sins.*

At this time, you might think, what is all of that have to do with **finding the path to life's purpose**? But if you look at what you have read so far, you will see that for some reason, we have lost it throughout time, and now we have a tremendous task before us to find that path. And to complicate things a lot more, we have so many choices to pick from! So many organizations offer the same thing. Some of them you know that they are way out of the path that the Bible shows us. And as a result of it, many people will be lost. How do I know this, you might ask? It has come to close in my own family. We have had some struggles about it, but many thanks to the Lord, we have prevailed. It was mainly with some of them that teach the Bible from their own interpretation until it became a cult, making them false teachers of the Bible. The bottom line here is that we have to be cautious about how to find the proper interpretations from the people we approach, and we have to make sure that they are closed to what the Bible has to say.

Here is where your own reading of the scriptures becomes handy. And be ready to decipher. And make sure of what you hear coincides with the Scriptures.

If you don't take it on your own to educate yourself about the scriptures (the Bible) and all the confusion that we have today, it is most likely you will end up with the wrong group of believers that profess to be Christians. Yet they are long ways from being one with the truth.

Christ has warned us about those kinds of people when He said in the book of *Mat. 7:15: Beware of false prophets, which come to you in sheep's clothing, but inwardly they are ravening wolves.*

Another good use of it is either self-education or having a Bible when you hear the scriptures being explained to you; you as the listener need to compare it yourself with what is being said. *Mat. 9:12: But when Jesus heard that, he said unto them, They that be whole need not a physician, but they that are sick. 13: But go ye and learn what that meaneth, I will have mercy, and not sacrifice: for I am not come to call the righteous, but sinners to repentance.*

This is an encounter that some of the so-called experts of that time should have known. What was Jesus saying to them? Yet He suggested to them to go and learn and compare about what He said with the scriptures. One of the problems with those people was that they had been so preoccupied adding some rules of their own, so much so that they were so confused among themselves; they could not see the difference when the truth was presented to them. This sounds very familiar today. Why don't we stick with His plan, instead of us trying to correct it, or modify it, like if we have more or better knowledge than He?

We have today so many different groups, organizations, or denominations that they are doing the same thing as those people did in the time of Christ, so much that they can't see the difference either and can't see that they are on the wrong path, and keep passing it along to others.

During my lifetime, I have been trying to be the best Christian I can be! Yet I have some encounters with similar people. Sometimes you hear some of them saying something that it does not sound right, naturally I have questioned it. Then I proceeded to ask if they can support it with the scriptures. I found that they did not have an answer, but they were surprised that I could question it, especially when the person I question was a minister of the gospel. The answer was, if it's good for those other people, then it is good enough for me. My reply was, even when whatever they said appears to be contrary to the scriptures, you would believe it? And they say yes, because it has been practiced for many years, so it must be okay.

Probably by now I got you curious! But there are several items that I have found that are very touching, like some want to bring the Old Testament into the Christian life of the New Testament; it will not work! Furthermore is that we now have divorce in our churches today as much as outside of the church. There are also several other things that add to the confusion. The sad part is that they all do it in the name of Christianity.

At this point, I like to get into the idea of bringing or combining the two testaments that some people think we need to keep. So far I have not found a place where the Bible says that God, or in this case Jesus, combined the two testaments together for us to keep in order to follow Him.

There is a reason why God came up with the New Testament, being that the people of that era could not keep. We read in the next verse, *Acts 15:10: Now therefore why tempt ye God, to put a yoke upon the neck of the disciples, which neither our fathers nor we were able to bear?*

He made it of a more inward application, and it does give way much better results, better desire within us to serve Him, and on a higher capacity than ever before. By that, I mean this! You probably have heard about the Ten Commandments. And according to some, they believe we need to keep.

They are composed of two parts.

First part 1 – Described in the first four commandments. They are called the vertical section, or should we say, between God and mankind. *Exodus 20:1: And God spake all these words, saying, 2: I am the LORD thy God, which have brought thee out of the land of Egypt, out of the house of bondage. 3: Thou shalt have no other gods before me. 4: Thou shalt not make unto thee any graven image, or any likeness of any thing that is in heaven above, or that is in the earth beneath, or that is in the water under the earth: 5: Thou shalt not bow down thyself to them, nor serve them: for I the LORD thy God am a jealous God, visiting the iniquity of the fathers upon the children unto the third and fourth generation of them that hate me; 6: And shewing mercy unto thousands of them that love me, and keep my commandments. 7: Thou shalt not take the name of the LORD thy God in vain; for the LORD will not hold him guiltless that taketh his name in vain.*

Second part 2 – The last six commandments are described as the parallel side, which is between humans, the relationship among us. Described in the next six commandments, *Exodus 20:*

8:   Remember the sabbath day, to keep it holy.

9:   Six days shalt thou labour, and do all thy work:

10:   But the seventh day is the sabbath of the LORD thy God: in it thou shalt not do any work, thou, nor thy son, nor thy daughter, thy manservant, nor thy maidservant, nor thy cattle, nor thy stranger that is within thy gates:

11:   For in six days the LORD made heaven and earth, the sea, and all that in them is, and rested the seventh day: wherefore the LORD blessed the sabbath day, and hallowed it.

12:   Honour thy father and thy mother: that thy days may be long upon the land which the LORD thy God giveth thee.

13:   Thou shalt not kill.

14:   Thou shalt not commit adultery.

15:   Thou shalt not steal.

16:   Thou shalt not bear false witness against thy neighbour.

17: Thou shalt not covet thy neighbour's house, thou shalt not covet thy neighbour's wife, nor his manservant, nor his maidservant, nor his ox, nor his ass, nor any thing that is thy neighbour's.

Now, let us make some observations to what Jesus Christ had to say in the New Testament when He quoted those passages and some of the commandments. Jesus shows us the difference that the Old has with the New when He says this in *Mathew 5:21: Ye have heard that it was said by them of old time, Thou shalt not kill; and whosoever shall kill shall be in danger of the judgment.*

He points the difference between then and now when He said,

22: But I say unto you, That whosoever is angry with his brother without a cause shall be in danger of the judgment: and whosoever shall say to his brother, Raca, shall be in danger of the council: but whosoever shall say, Thou fool, shall be in danger of hell fire.

So the THOU SHALT NOT KILL, referring to the sixth commandment found in the Old Testament, Exodus 20:13 and Mathew 5 above when He said that whosoever is angry with his brother shall be in danger of the judgment, and whosoever shall say to his brother, Raca, shall be in danger of the council. Let's observe on what the differences are. The difference is that Jesus is getting to the root of the problem! By cultivating that anger instead of stopping it, and keep it from escalating, and being that anger, is what drives a person to the place to where they want to kill, and ultimately killing the one that provoked you to anger.

When we apply it based on the Old Testament, you can get as angry with someone, and go as far as calling that person anything or any names or whatever comes to your mind, but as long as you don't kill, you are okay. Under the New Testament, or more specific in Mathew 5:21 above, Jesus is telling us that all starts when you begin to get upset with someone, then you start to get mad! It escalates to anger. And that needs to stop right there. Because if you continue to feed and nourish that anger, it will become uncontrollable and can lead to killing, and as a rule, it will not get any better for as long as you keep cultivating that anger, it will get worse. The point here is that this person is getting angrier by the minute, it did not stop it, and it got out of hand. As you probably already know, lots of people cannot control anger, and as a result, it can escalate to the point where many, therefore, will become killers.

Jesus describes to us the root of the problem. By keeping us from getting upset, and if we do, we need to stop before we get real mad, and from the place of anger that can lead us to killing. The proper thing to do here is not to get angry and not give any room to anger. Because it can escalate to where you can lose control over it. We have then a choice to make, and that is to turn around and walk away from the problem. It was here that finally I understood what my grandma used to tell me! She used to say it is more macho (tough) for the one that runs than the one that stays. I never understood what she meant until I read this passage.

So under the Old Testament, you can get angry and still have not sin. But under the New Testament, if you get mad, you can sin before you kill. Therefore, you cannot live under the Old Testament rules or, more specific, the Ten Commandments as a Christian because you will sin even before you kill. More clearly: the Ten Commandments are not for Christians to live by.

The next one, Ex. 20:14 above, is similar: **THOU SHALT NOT COMMIT ADULTERY.** This is under the Old Testament.

Pointing to the Old Testament, Jesus said in *Matthew 5:27: Ye have heard that it was said by them of old time, Thou shalt not commit adultery.*

Now in the New Testament, Jesus is pointing to us the difference in *Matthew 5:28: But I say unto you, That whosoever looketh on a woman to lust after her hath committed adultery with her already in his heart.*

He is telling us where the problem has its origin. This passage tells us that this person is doing more than just looking, by developing a plane to carry out its evil thoughts, and that is quite different than the one in the Old Testament. Under the Old Testament, you haven't sin until you commit the act, or have sex outside marriage. But Jesus is telling us that under the New Testament, before you get to that place of committing adultery or cheating, you have already committed sin. Therefore, you as a Christian cannot go by the Ten Commandments, and still be a Christian. You will sin even before you commit the act. You will be living under sin, but also living a hypocrite life, even when you have not committed adultery, according to the Old Testament. Being this the difference, and reason for the change from the Old to the New Testament. (One little observation: This command of **Adultery** is applicable only to married individuals. **Fornication** is for on-married people or singles. It is used for a man and a woman engaged to be married.) Engagement is also considered sacred in the Eyes of God, so therefore, you cannot cheat on your fiancé, or the one you have promised to be married to.

Now! Based on this commandment, God does not want anything to happen to those that have declared to the world that they have been united in matrimony before God Himself. *Mt 19:6: Wherefore they are no more twain, but one flesh. What therefore God hath joined together, let not man put asunder.*

He considers this union to be sacred and optimally is a contract between a man and a woman, and it is not to be tempered with, meaning, that a married person can't cheat and can't break that contract. So when you get married, it is onetime only, or until one of the spouses passes away based on this next verse. *1 Co.7:39: The wife is bound by the law as long as her husband liveth; but if her husband be dead, she is at liberty to be married to whom she will; only in the Lord.*

Now! What makes a married person wanting to terminate this union and cheats? The obvious answer is that it is sin that dwells in or around us. The problem then is, when a person looks to the opposite sex, and dwells on the notion, to where and how to bring it to pass **(looked on a woman to lust after her)**, meaning that just looking is not the problem, it is dwelling on the thoughts that can lead to disaster. And that is where the problem starts according to Jesus. When you cultivate a bad thought and the purpose is to bring it to pass.

Here is one more of several changes that Jesus made in the New Testament. In *Jn 4:20: Our fathers worshipped in this mountain; and ye* say, that in Jerusalem is the place where men ought to worship. *Jn 4:21*

Jesus saith unto her, Woman, believe me, the hour cometh, when ye shall neither in this mountain, nor yet at Jerusalem, worship the Father.

Jesus on his conversation with the woman by the well, He is telling her how they were allowed to worship is now changed. The change is that before, or in the Old Testament, they were required to worship in one location, geographically. But now you can worship in the Spirit, anywhere in the world not just in Jerusalem, as they were required to do so.

Based on those commandments, the people of the Old Testament could not put two and two together. They were not able to keep them. This is the reason why God gave us the New Testament, by making it a little more personal.

This is one of the things Jesus does for us when we become his followers or should we say Christians. As part of our conversion or getting saved as it is called, He will get rid of the original sin that cusses us to commit sin and do the unthinkable things that the original sin drives us to do.

Another observation we need to make is that God did not make us to become sinners! It was Satan that got into the picture, and therefore now we are born in sin. This is the only reason for Christ to go to all the measures to get us back to His original intent, not wanting for us to go to hell. That was prepared for Satan and his angels, says *Mathew 25:41: Then shall he say also unto them on the left hand, Depart from me, ye cursed, into everlasting fire, prepared for the devil and his angels:*

As you can see, what He wants for us is to take us and bring us to where He is, and as a reward for our obedience, eternal life with Him forever. Just in case you did not notice it, there are only four commandments between God and man, and six between us and our fellowman. Then Jesus reduced them into two. One for each, when He said in *Mathew 22:37: Jesus said unto him, Thou shalt love the Lord thy God with all thy heart, and with all thy soul, and with all thy mind.*

38: This is the first and great commandment.

39: And the second is like unto it, Thou shalt love thy neighbour as thyself.

40: On these two commandments hang all the law and the prophets.

All come down to this, that the key to all of the above is LOVE! And it could not get any simpler then to be able to understand it (love) and learn how to apply it to our life, to be successful Christians. NOTE: In the Greek language, there are different words that described our one-word *Love*. Each one of them is translated love, yet there are different kinds of what we call love: (1) The word *Agape*, it is used here to describe love between man and God. (2) The word *Philia*, which describes the love between humans, and where they got the name for the city of Philadelphia, meaning the **City of Brotherly Love**.

There is another thought that we like to explore for a moment. And that is about why we have the need for rules or commandments to be bothered with. As you know, most people do not like to live under rules, and some of them go as far as hating them. They would prefer to be lawless. So let's look at what would happen if people would live without any law and, if there are any consequences, if law is out of the picture.

Let's see what would happen if there were no rules that said, Do not kill. Assuming for a moment that one member of Family 1 kills a member of Family 2. Then there is nothing that can keep Family 2 to seek revenge and go over and maybe wipe out several members of Family 1, or vice versa. If that could keep up, we probably could wipe out our entire human race. That still does happen sometimes, even when there are laws that prevent it.

The other is, When there is nothing that says, Thou shalt not commit adultery, meaning, that you have the liberty to do as you please, you can go and sleep around with anyone you want. What happens then? Your partner and your children would not be pleased with your behavior. Let's say that you decided to change partners, then you end up displeasing the other. As a rule, the displeased one would be insulted and can escalate to the place of wanting to eliminate that person by committing murder. That also still does happen, even when we have laws that govern over it.

Here is one more: and that is the one that says, Thou shalt not steal. You know that everyone does not like when they are robbed of anything they possess or work hard for. Not even among thieves. I have never met anyone that said that they were so happy that they got robbed of their precious possessions. Any of those things mentioned above is not in our nature to tolerate them.

They are just simply unacceptable and plain wrong. The same here, stealing is probably the most common thing around us, even when they know they are going to be caught or to get arrested and sent to jail. Some have given their life for it.

People are driven to do some of those things, and they are trying to fill an emptiness we have in ourselves that only God can fulfil. We try to fill it in our own anyway, and many times with the wrong thing. The one so-called human love, hate, or anything that is at our disposal, yet nothing seems to fulfill it. And nothing can except God himself.

Now God has given us a better way to fulfill that empty spot or place that we have in our nature that only Him can occupy. You probably have experienced it, or at least have heard about an emptiness we have in our lives, that no matter what we do, it cannot be satisfied, because it is His to occupy only. People try to satisfy it, one way or another, with money, possessions, and many times with the wrong kinds of pleasures. The bad news is that you can't fill it with any other than the Grace and Love of God. *Romans 10:10: For with the heart man believeth unto righteousness; and with the mouth confession is made unto salvation.*

And that is how you can fulfill that emptiness by believing and confessing our sins. This process has been designed to restore our relationship with our maker in order to have Him occupy that empty spot in our heart that He designed for Himself only.

Apparently this is an area that can be tempered with! Our (Heart/Mind) Satan either knows or discovers it, and tries to occupy it, and has been very successful at it. The scriptures refer to it as the Heart, not the physical part, but the spiritual one, or the center of the human life (Heart/Mind). Many believe it to be the mind because that is there where all of those things are processed and also where we rationalized all that we encounter, or all of our decisions are made at. Let's compare it to a robot that uses a computer chip or processor that makes it perform all the tasks that it does. And being this the part in need of repair.

In other words, it needs to have a complete overhaul by the creator of it, which in this case, the only one qualified to perform the necessary repairs is God Himself. He is the only one who brings it to its original specs. No one other than the designer and creator can do this. In this case, God Himself being our creator, He is the only one qualified to restore it to its original state. We know that Satan has tempered with it, and we also have found ways to temper with it (our mind). But all Satan and we have done is made a mess of it.

Not for a moment ever think that you can do or have someone perform that operation to you. No one can but God Himself who is the original designer. *Romans 2:29: But he is a Jew, which is one inwardly; and circumcision is that of the heart, in the spirit, and not in the letter; whose praise is not of men, but of God.*

Talking about circumcision, it means to cut off or remove unwanted items, things that will interfere with the functions and proper behavior of it. Continuing to describe that location in the human body, we can see, and apparently it is not talking of the physical heart. Also, depending on the things or who occupies it. This will bring forth and see what the next verses are telling us. *Mathew 15:19: For out of the heart proceed evil thoughts, murders, adulteries, fornications, thefts, false witness, blasphemies; Mark 7:21: For from within, out of the heart of men, proceed evil thoughts, adulteries, fornications, murders; Mathew 12:34 O generation of vipers, how can ye, being evil, speak goodthings? for out of the abundance of the heart the mouth speaketh.*

Where do you find all of those items mentioned above? Appears to be the mind, based on whatever is stored in it, or who possesses it. It will dictate how you will behave with others. This has been one of the ways that gives you away as a Christian, by the way you think, talk, and conduct yourself. But also there are people that without being Christians, they appear to act like one, having good manners and of an overall superior conduct. In fact, I used to have an aunt of mine that looked and acted like a holiness lady, or a saint, like some people probably will describe them to be, and acted better than most Christians I know. In great part, I think that it has to do with the way they are brought up, and the examples they have from the parents and people around them, but still have the need of Christ.

Just because you have or possess some of those qualities does not exempt you from the Salvation that Christ is offering to us. We all are born sinners and need God's forgiveness. *Romans 3:9: What then? are we better than they? No, in no wise: for we have before proved both Jews and Gentiles, that they are all under sin. 1 Tim. 1:15: This is a faithful saying, and worthy of all acceptation, that Christ Jesus came into the world to save sinners; of whom I am chief.*

Up to this point, we have been talking of the different phases that are affected as we go through life that in one time or another we encounter in our lifetime. The one thing we need to emphasize is this item we call life that we possess or have the privilege to have been entrusted with and has been given to us to manage. It is irreplaceable, and it's been given to us unfortunately only once, meaning, that if there is anything you cannot make with, it would be too many mistakes. You will end up making a mess of it, or even as far as losing it. The one thing to remember is that it is only one life, one time, that was given to us. Therefore, together with the physical body, they both need all the necessary precautions we can give it and manage them with and certain kind of delicate and loving care. Remember that we only have or been given one of each and are inseparable. These three items (Body, Soul, and Spirit) are what makes us, or you as an individual, unique and different from any other. But the most important thing to remember is that they are irreplaceable. Design to reflect you only and is unmistakable. And neither one can co-exist without the other, or until God decides to give you a spiritual body.
1 Co. 15:44: It is sown a natural body; it is raised a spiritual body. There is a natural body, and there is a spiritual body.

Sad to say, but in our society of today, we have very little regard for either of them (life/body), so much so that we either know or hear of someone that had their life cut off so early. But more surprisingly is when it is done through self-inflicted terminal illness or homicide, meaning, that in any of those cases, they don't have any regard for life, or the life of others.

Also a big percentage of people go as far as saying that they don't like the way they look. You hear about people spending great amount of money trying to change their appearance to their own satisfaction. Rather we should be spending our time taking care of what we got. We can make some improvements to it, but it should be without altering the original. For example, by dressing, it does change our appearance and make us feel better, but it should be in modesty and not making ourselves ridiculous.Remember that we are not only God's restored individuals, but also we do represent and reflect Him in the way we look and whatever we do or say. *Philippians 4:5: Let your moderation be known unto all men. The Lord is at hand.*

What makes people dissatisfied with either their life or their body or the way they look? The answer here is different for most cases, but the results are the same, and it's not being happy with one's self, the way we see our own life or body. It is like telling God that He made a mistake when He created us. *Gen 2:7: And the LORD God formed man of the dust of the ground, and breathed into his nostrils the breath of life; and man became a living soul.*

The way we look is really up to us, by taking care of whatever we got, the way we dress it and the way we nourish it. There are people that become so dissatisfied with themselves so much that they like to end it all.

Somewhere in life we either took the wrong turn or have been handed the wrong influence or teachings. If we were to trace it back, you will find that as time goes by, people have very little respect for life, especially in our lifetime, it seems to be worse than ever before. Today we have very little regard when it comes to life, appearance, respect, and the language we speak (too many bad words in our vocabulary). The good news is that as we read above, there is one thing we can do and change the direction of where our life or body is going. Remember it was mentioned above that it can be tempered with? But in order to keep it simple, we need to stop and analyze the direction we are going, and then see what steps we need to take and make sure that we are going in the right path, humanly, morally, and overall, biblically. Otherwise we will miss the point altogether again, and all we do is go from bad to worse. The best is for us to take advantage of the path that God already has laid out for us and follow it.

Whenever we take it on our own in solving problems that only God can, it's here where we will miss the point. It is altogether different when we allow our own creator to do what is best for our life. Don't you think that He can do a better job than we could ever do? Besides, of all the obstacles that we confront all the time, without Him, it is impossible to decipher all the bad elements from the good. As Humans, we need help, with guidance on which direction to go, especially on spiritual discernment. It can get very confusing if we don't follow His road map (the Bible) that He has already provided for us. *2 Tm. 2:15: Study to shew thyself approved unto God, a workman that needeth not to be ashamed, rightly dividing the word of truth.*

With all of this in mind, we will go into the next phase for our journey to **finding the path for our own life**. There are a couple of steps we need to cover in order for us to find the purpose of life and make sure we are on the right track that God already laid out for us to follow.

SOME GUIDELINES AS WE GET STARTED

God has been so faithful and fair to us and wants us to weigh all the costs and to follow his instructions by painting a picture before us about what will be ahead as we try to **find the path for our life** with His help. *Luc. 14:26: If any man come to me, and hate not his father, and mother, and wife, and children, and brethren, and sisters, yea, and his own life also, he cannot be my disciple.*
27: And whosoever doth not bear his cross, and come after me, cannot be my disciple.

28: For which of you, intending to build a tower, sitteth not down first, and counteth the cost, whether he have sufficient to finish it?
29: Lest haply, after he hath laid the foundation, and is not able to finish it, all that behold it begin to mock him,
30: Saying, This man began to build, and was not able to finish.

Jesus is telling us in verse 26, by using a metaphor to describe how important it is for a person to redirect his/hers priorities, by showing them that in order to accomplish this task is the same as if you hate someone. As a result of that hate, you will direct your love to someone else. Jesus is saying that in order for us to be His disciples, we need to put Him first and above all others in our life, not second place, but first. In verses 28 to 30, He tells the story of this man that was going to build a tower. He needs to consider the cost needed to build it before he starts his project, otherwise he will be made fun of for not finishing what he started. This also applies to anyone who is considering on becoming a Christian, meaning, are we willing to go all the way with Christ? Otherwise, best not to start something we know we will not finish. Or, as mentioned before, doing it our way will also be a failure. It is sad and shameful! But there are a lot of those out there wanting to be Christians on their own terms. Now, how do we know this? This next verse will explain it. *Mat. 7:20: Wherefore by their fruits ye shall know them.*

(We as Christians need to produce good fruit.)

And as you look around, there are some Christians that are not able to produce the right fruit, and in many cases, they will go contrary to the scriptures. As long as they are alive, they have the option to either do it in God's way, or best to leave it alone and not to send the wrong impressions that you can do anything you want and still be a Christian.

The sad part is that not only you have deceived yourself by malpractice of God's commandments, but also you will drag others with you and will cause them to go in the wrong path as well. In this case, you need to better examine yourselves and make sure you are following His path by the scriptures as closest as you can.

That is why He has given us the ability to be able to choose Him. He is looking for genuine followers and servants of Himself and His kingdom. You can't follow Christ by picking only the things you think that apply to yourself, or they are more appropriate for the lifestyle you now have, and still think you can accomplish it anyway as you see it fit.

Whenever anybody tries to follow someone else's route or examples without checking it, you need to make sure you're doing the right thing, otherwise, you will find yourself going in the same direction as they are. Especially when you decide to ignore it and try to make changes to the original commandment to fit your own taste.

In this case, you will end up being something else other than what was intended for you to be. Usually, it happens when you don't follow the directions made and given to you by Christ, or by not following His commandments. They are not to be misinterpreted and tempered with to fit your taste or your own lifestyle; it is best to leave them as they are. The proper thing is to follow them as they are, or better leave them alone.

NOW OUR RESPONSE TO HIS CALLING

Romans 10:14: How then shall they call on him in whom they have not believed? And how shall they believe in him of whom they have not heard? And how shall they hear without a preacher?

In our time, especially today, we have a number of ways in which we can hear the Gospel. There is radio, AM, FM, or shortwave radio that, for me, I enjoy the best; we have local television or by satellite, but also other ways like computers and the Internet, and now smartphones.

All of this is done either at the comfort of your home or even in your vehicle (if it happens that you drive one). Besides all of those, we still read books, and you can hear it in person if you choose to do so by attending Church and sometimes other church special events.

With all those choices, it leaves very little room for excuses not to hear the Good News that we all need at least once in our lifetime. It will take us to that place that we need to be into. Maybe will take us to the beginning of our journey in finding the way and purpose of our life.

Talking about excuses, I have asked this question. As of now, you haven't accepted Christ as your Savior? Surprisingly, I heard several reasons for not becoming a Christian: (1) because they said that there are too many rules; (2) too many do's and don'ts and so on. Naturally I had to ask, what is there that you can do that I can't as a Christian? The most common answer is, can't drink (alcoholic beverages) or smoke cigarettes. My response to this was, based on my own experience that I had with cigarettes, I discover this before I became a Christian; that some of those things you are craving for are not beneficial to you and your health. The reason for not drinking is, I have seen the effect that it has on people who drink, especially when they can't control the amount they are able to consume. It makes that person lose their ability to act sane, and it makes them appear to be other than what they really are or supposed to be.

But most important is that I have seen many of them end their life cut shorter than it should as a result of alcoholism. So why would I go after something that will cause me to even lose my life over it? On the other hand, when I started to keep up with the older boys by smoking, I found out what cigarettes are capable of, also what it was doing to me.

I discovered it when I used to ride my bicycle regularly on this road that has several different-sized hills and went through this road many times. Then, in one of those times, I ran out of air in the middle of this one small hill and could not continue riding it as usual to the top of the hill. I had to get off my bike and walk the rest of it. That got my attention and made me feel a little concerned and puzzled at the same time. And in one of those times I was carrying a pack of cigarette in my shirt pocket that I started to smoke and had been smoking for about a week. I knew that this had to be the problem, because up to this time, that is the only thing I have done out of the ordinary. So I decided to stop smoking them. It took about a week before I could go up that hill again. I also noticed that it took me that long before clearing out my system. Naturally, I had to make sure that the cigarettes were the problem, so I started to smoke again; and sure enough, it happened again! But this time I knew for sure that the cigarettes were the problem. So I pulled that pack of cigarettes out of my pocket and tossed it into the bushes as far as I could throw it. As a result, I have never touched cigarettes ever again; or since then. The same principle you can apply with other things, such as drugs, sex, etc.

My answer to those people was when it comes to drinking and smoking, the only thing they do is to damage oneself, physically and spiritually. And for some reason, people go after those things even when they know of the damage that comes by consuming them.

I also have mentioned to them that when it comes to obeying rules, sometimes you need to find out for yourself, in order to be convinced of it. In this case, I found out on my own that some of those rules are there for my own benefit, and many times, for my own protection.

I also have asked myself that question! What is there that they can do that I can't? So I asked them the same question. What is there that you can do that I can't? The answer there is none. If I don't practice some of the things you do, it is because I have found out for myself that what those things do for me is damage my health. That is why, Jesus does not want us or me in this case to get into and practice them. He wants us to go through life sanely and to enjoy it to the fullness and perhaps live longer.

The same goes for the rest of the others like cheating, stealing, hating, lying, etc. The bottom line is that there is nothing that they can do that you or I can't. The only difference of why I do not practice any of those things is, first, Jesus said not to. Second, they are harmful to us, and they are very damaging to those who consume or practice them. You either commit sin or get sick in the process. You will be putting your life on the line but also risking everything.

Up to now we have covered pretty much everything we need to know and about how to find that place where we ought to be and should be in order for us to live the kind of life that God intended and wants us to have and find the **real purpose of our life**.

Now we will go into the next chapter and cover how to find that path and essentially find out how to know Christ and establish a real genuine relationship with Him. He already made His, and now He is waiting for us to make our move. He will do all He can with all His power to help us become the best in our selves. Remember, what we are pursuing is a relationship with Christ, and not religion. This will make a great difference in our endeavor to pursue life as it was meant for us to be.

||||||||||||||||||||||||

PART ONE

PHASE NUMBER TWO

WHO CAN BE SAVED?

Is Salvation for everyone? Who can be saved? Anybody? The answer is no! (1) Because there are some requirements to be fulfilled or you will not get saved. You might think or say, I heard! And is it not true that Christ died for all mankind? Isn't Salvation for everyone? The answer is yes! (2) But before you get saved, you need to be called by Him. *Jn. 6:44: No man can come to me, except the Father which hath sent me draw him: and I will raise him up at the last day.*

And not everyone who gets called will respond to His calling. Next, you will need to know: (1) What salvation is!; (2) What is it for?; and, (3) If you need it, now we will find out, HOW TO GET SAVED.

We will be discussing what steps are needed and what takes place when a person gets saved. Let's call those steps, ingredients, for the sake of identifying those that are required for this purpose.

There are three questions we need to answer before we can proceed.

We need to define (1) **What is Salvation!**; (2) **What is it for?**; and, (3) **Do we need it?**

1)   What is Salvation?

Defined by a dictionary: **it is the liberation from the power and the effects of Sin.** But in order to have a better understanding on how all of these came into existence, we need to read God's word. Somewhere in time, God decided to make what we now know is our world, and all the things in it, including mankind. Somehow Satan already existed as a fallen angel. *2 Pt 2:4: For if God spared not the angels that sinned, but cast them down to hell, and delivered them into chains of darkness, to be reserved unto judgment.*

Then after He created everything else, God decided to create man and woman, or should we say, Adam and Eve. *Genesis 1:26: And God said, Let us make man in our image, after our likeness: and let them have dominion over the fish of the sea, and over the fowl of the air, and over the cattle, and over all the earth, and over every creeping thing that creepeth upon the earth.*

27:   So God created man in his own image, in the image of God created he him; male and female created he them.

28:   And God blessed them, and God said unto them, Be fruitful, and multiply, and replenish the earth, and subdue it: and have dominion over the fish of the sea, and over the fowl of the air, and over every living thing that moveth upon the earth.

29:   And God said, Behold, I have given you every herb bearing seed, which is upon the face of all the earth, and every tree, in the which is the fruit of a tree yielding seed; to you it shall be for meat.

30:   And to every beast of the earth, and to every fowl of the air, and to every thing that creepeth upon the earth, wherein there is life, I have given every green herb for meat: and it was so.

31:   And God saw every thing that he had made, and, behold, it was very good.

And the evening and the morning were the sixth day.

God then made a special garden to put Adam and Eve and told them to be the keeper of it. This garden came with one exception: Not to eat from the tree of knowledge. *Gen 2:7: And the LORD God formed man of the dust of the ground, and breathed into his nostrils the breath of life; and man became a living soul.*

8: *And the LORD God planted a garden eastward in Eden; and there he put the man whom he had formed. 15: And the LORD God took the man, and put him into the garden of Eden to dress it and to keep it.*

16: *And the LORD God commanded the man, saying, Of every tree of the garden thou mayest freely eat:*

17: *But of the tree of the knowledge of good and evil, thou shalt not eat of it: for in the day that thou eatest thereof thou shalt surely die.*

It was here where they were tempted by the serpent or Satan. *Gen 3:13: And the LORD God said unto the woman, What is this that* thou hast done? And the woman said, The serpent beguiled me, and I did eat. *Gen 2:17 And unto Adam he said, Because thou hast hearkened unto the voice of thy wife, and hast eaten of the tree, of which I commanded thee, saying, Thou shalt not eat of it: cursed is the ground for thy sake; in sorrow shalt thou eat of it all the days of thy life.*

This is where we find the reason for the fall of man, by simply disobeying an order that God had given to Adam. Then God had to punish both of them, Adam and Eve, by putting them out of the garden.

Gen 3:23: Therefore the LORD God sent him forth from the garden of Eden, to till the ground from whence he was taken.

Therefore, now man has to be rescued or be saved from his own mistake. But God had already designed a plan to bring man out from sin. Nevertheless, man still is the center of it, and all revolve around for the purpose of man. Man is God's precious creation and possession, so much so that He has gone as far as sacrificing His only begotten Son in order to preserve mankind, as the Scripture tell us in *John 3:16: For*

God so loved the world, that he gave his only begotten Son, that whosoever believeth in him should not perish, but have everlasting life.

2)   What is it for?

As we can see Salvation, its purpose is to restore what once got lost as man was put on this world, and he (man) got deceived by the serpent or Satan *2 Cor 11:3: But I fear, lest by any means, as the serpent beguiled Eve through his subtilty, so your minds should be corrupted from the simplicity that is in Christ.*

He took the form of a serpent in order to do his trick, *Rv 12:9: And the great dragon was cast out, that old serpent, called the Devil, and Satan, which deceiveth the whole world: he was cast out into the earth, and his angels were cast out with him.*

And because of man, Salvation has been put into place in order to restore what got lost in the Garden of Eden. God's original plan that was designed even before all of this got started. *Ti 1:2: In hope of eternal life, which God, that cannot lie, promised before the world began;*

Salvation came into place when man fell, but it got a little more complicated, when man has sons and daughters. They are now born in sin, and now they can commit sins of their own as we discuss it above.

Now, God is doing everything in His power to bring it all to its original intent, without us being force; and start that wonderful family of His own. *2 Co. 17: Wherefore come out from among them, and be ye separate, saith the Lord, and touch not the unclean thing; and I will receive you, 18: And will be a Father unto you, and ye shall be my sons and daughters, saith the Lord Almighty.*

Heb. 8:10: For this is the covenant that I will make with the house of Israel after those days, saith the Lord; I will put my laws into their mind, and write them in their hearts: and I will be to them a God, and they shall be to me a people:

3) **Do we need it?**

This is where the FREE WILL that God bestowed upon us comes into play. I think it is pretty obvious that salvation as we just saw it, we do need it, and God has provided it for us to take advantage of. The one thing that we need to remember is this: It's FREE and is not being forced on anyone. God has given mankind the ability to make decisions of their own, *Deut 30:19: I call heaven and earth to record this day against you, that I have set before you life and death, blessing and cursing: therefore choose life, that both thou and thy seed may live:*

It could not be any plainer than this, black and white. We have been given, and there are two choices to pick from. We will either choose LIFE or DEATH. Isn't it so obvious that out of the two anybody wouldn't pick death? Yet this is what most people end up choosing. The question is why. But by now you probably can answer that. We have an enemy that is constantly enticing mankind with all sorts of things that appear to be good to the eye and sweet music to the ear even when we know that at the end. It will take us to destruction. E.g., For starters, by going to jail, getting real sick, bringing discomfort to other people, or relatives, and in some cases, at the cost of our own life, or the life of others. Yet we pursue the bad things that come across our path. But like other things, there comes the time when you need to decide if it is for you or not! Salvation, that is. And how do you go about getting it?

First, *John 6:65: And he said, Therefore said I unto you, that no man can come unto me, except it were given unto him of my Father.*

We all are called, and God somehow sees that everyone gets notified that there are only two choices, through which we will have to pick from; it'll be one or the other. There is no middle groun. Good or evil. *1Co. 7:17: But as God hath distributed to every man, as the Lord hath called every one, so let him walk. And so ordain I in all churches.*

But how is it that not everyone gets save? *Mt 7:13: Enter ye in at the strait gate: for wide is the gate, and broad is the way, that leadeth to destruction, and many there be which go in thereat:*

We just read that most people go to the wide path that leads to destruction. Bottom line is that most will take the wrong way and pass up on eternal life for something so called good times, or a short time of thrills, or glamorous fame. Note: There is nothing wrong with any of those things if they are done under God's approval. He wants us to enjoy life to its fullest and still remain blameless. *Eccl 3:13: And also that every man should eat and drink, and enjoy the good of all his labour, it is the gift of God.*

With this in mind, let's pursue it with more serious intentions and with approval of Him who gives us all of those things, including life. Let us not forget that God, in all of His ways, wants nothing but the best for all His children.

NEXT, THE FIVE INGREDIENTS

Up to this time, we have established the necessary path to go forward and continue to our objective in order to fulfil God's requirements. We still have to cover several steps that I call ingredients which we need in order to make sure we are on the right track. When we are all done with it, we will know where we stand and make sure that we are and remain with assurance that we are in the center of God's will.

#1 FAITH – What is faith? *He. 11:1: Now faith is the substance of things hoped for, the evidence of things not seen.*

With this self-explanatory verse, we can see that faith is a very important ingredient we need in order to proceed. *Heb. 11:6: But without faith it is impossible to please him: for he that cometh to God must believe that he is, and that he is a rewarder of them that diligently seek him.*

My hope is that by now, we have built our faith to the place where we can put it into practice. We are going to need it to believe in God and Jesus Christ whom He sent to take our place at Calvary and die in our place, and from there, we attain Grace through Jesus our Savior. But to make it a little more concrete, we read in *John 20:30: And many other signs truly did Jesus in the presence of his disciples, which are not written in this book: 31: But these are written, that ye might believe that Jesus is the Christ, the Son of God; and that believing ye might have life through his name.*

Therefore faith is an essential ingredient and we can obtain it by hearing the word, *Rom. 10:17: So then faith cometh by hearing, and hearing by the word of God.* All we need is to apply it to ourselves to bring out the next ingredient.

#2 CONVICTION – Based on a dictionary definition, it is **being convinced or fully awakened to awareness**. We have a very good illustration in the story of the Prodigal Son. *Luc. 15:17: And when he came to himself, he said, How many hired servants of my father's have bread enough and to spare, and I perish with hunger! 18: I will arise and go to my father, and will say unto him, Father, I have sinned against heaven, and before thee, 19: And am no more worthy to be called thy son: make me as one of thy hired servants.*

Having conviction will allow us to take a good look at ourselves. Then after analyzing oneself, we will be able to see if we qualified to be servants of Christ or not. All we need to start with is recognizing and admitting that we have sin. That is what conviction does for us; it shows us where we stand and helps us to see that we are sinners and that we need Christ's forgiveness. But also it will make us understand that we need repentance. If we fail to recognize that we are sinners, then we will have nothing to forsake and repent from. There will be no need for confession, and no need for salvation either.

Keep in mind that *Rom 3:23: For all have sinned, and come short of the glory of God.*

#3 FORSAKE – By definition, it is **to leave or withdraw from; to depart, to renounce, to abandon, and to reject.** Once we have dealt with conviction, there will be a change, and we need to get ready to forsake our way of life as we know it. At this point, we are at a position where we are willing to leave all behind and ready to make that change in our life. *Luc 9:23: And he said to them all, If any man will come after me, let him deny himself, and take up his cross daily, and follow me. Luc. 14:33: So likewise, whosoever he be of you that forsaketh not all that he hath, he cannot be my disciple.*

What we learn from these verses is that we need to set our priorities in a proper perspective and render what is due to Him (Jesus). Before we will go to Him and ask for forgiveness, we have to make sure that we are prepared to make that commitment and that we are going to serve Him on His terms. Although this might sound like an impossible task to you, it is not! All we are doing at this point is making sure that we are ready to commit our life to Christ with a genuine heart and to avoid being just a superficial act. We need a real change of heart that will stand the challenges of time as we start a new life in Christ, leaving it all behind, including bad habits, and just focus **on that purpose of our new life**, as some people have said, "Burning all the bridges behind us."

Remember that it is God we are dealing with. You might be able to fool anybody else or yourself, but you will not be able to fool Him. He will know if you are for real or not.

#4 REPENT – It's defined **to feel such sorrow for one's sins as to reform.** *Mark 1:15b: And saying, The time is fulfilled, and the kingdom of God is at hand: repent ye, and believe the gospel. Acts. 3:19a Repent ye therefore, and be converted, that your sins may be blotted out, when the times of refreshing shall come from the presence of the Lord; Acts 11:18b: When they heard these things, they held their peace, and glorified God, saying, Then hath God also to the Gentiles granted repentance unto life.*

Now that we have understood what is involved in the previous ingredient or number 3, we are now ready to repent from our sins and be able to tell God that we are ready to repent and are sorry for what we have done in our past and the sins we have committed as a person that has been practicing the wrong things contrary to His will. Not just some things, but all wrongdoings we have done.

Repentance has to be real genuine action from our heart and mind, such a real repentance that will not be so easily moved as to go back and continue to practice our bad habits, making us nothing more than hypocrites. But now we want to be able to go to God and tell Him that we mean business and that we are ready for His forgiveness, ready to live a clean life, capable of reflecting Him on all we do and say.

Now the last and final ingredient!

#5 CONFESSION – It is **to acknowledge or admit to someone, as a fault, guilt, or debt, to acknowledge belief or faith in.**
Rom. 10:9: That if thou shalt confess with thy mouth the Lord Jesus, and shalt believe in thine heart that God hath raised him from the dead, thou shalt be saved. :10 For with the heart man believeth unto righteousness; and with the mouth confession is made unto salvation.

Even though this is one of those items, we know God knows, *Mat. 6:8: Be not ye therefore like unto them: for your Father knoweth what things ye have need of, before ye ask him.*

As far as Confession is concern, I have pointed the most common sins, but keep in mind that there are people who find themselves sometimes in particularly unusual circumstances. Keep in mind that not all of us commit the same sins. God with all His faithfulness will point to you those items at a proper time, so be prepared for God's check, He will bring to your attention the areas in your life that need correction.

This is a procedure or requirement He wants us to perform that involves several items such as Believe with our hearts/minds, of Christ's resurrection, and words coming out of our mouth, meaning that not only we have acknowledged and are aware of our position and having processed faith, conviction, forsakenness, and repentance in our mind. We have found all we know of ourselves where we stand, and we are ready to proceed and confess our sins to Him, knowing that He is there ready to forgive us. But not until then we will be saved. *1 John 1:9: If we confess our sins, he is faithful and just to forgive us our sins, and to cleanse us from all unrighteousness.*

There is a problem among people when it comes to asking for forgiveness or to ask for an apology to others. Somehow, it is hard for most to admit guilt. It is really hard to admit that we have done someone wrong and really mean it when it comes to making apologies. Many times we just do it to acquire sympathy or favoritism from other people. Expressing sorrow for what we done, in some cases, is that our heart is not in it and our mind is far from it. As a rule, we just want to say what others expect from us. This will not work when it comes to confessing our sins to God. We read above that He knows what our intentions are even before we ask Him. What does that mean for us? It means that we have to be genuine, be real, and be sincere. Otherwise, all of our endeavors will be for nothing; and all of the procedures were nothing but poor performance.

One of the things that helps in this case is, we have to understand who God really is. And go to Him as such: the supreme King, worth of our worship, who has allowed us to be in His presence, with a sincere heart that is willing to serve Him with all we got. He needs to be in first place in our life.

God, knowing our weaknesses, suggests to us that we need to make sure that we know what we're getting into before we come to this point. Let us not treat it like a game we can play with, after all, it is our life we are dealing with, giving us chance to make it better; and ultimately eternal life with Him forever. *1 John 2:25: And this is the promise that he hath promised us, even eternal life.*

Once you go through this last ingredient, as I call them, and do it properly, you will be saved. It is here where your new life begins! And all your family, friends, and coworkers will have a new person in their life. THIS calls for a time of celebration, even in heaven. *Lk. 15:10: Likewise, I say unto you, there is joy in the presence of the angels of God over one sinner that repenteth.*

Then you need to tell the world of the change that just happened in your life. Now next step is to get baptized with water, as part of your conversion, which I will describe in the next step or chapter.

After covering all the steps described above, it is not as complicated as it appears to be. All of that comes together in an instant when it comes to getting save. But it is way easier to do when you know what steps to take. It will ensure the success of your conversion. Plus, it will be easier for you to help someone when the time comes.

CHAPTER TWO

PART TWO

THE BAPTISM OF WATER

This is one of the ingredients that is part of the previous step, yet is somehow separated from it. It does take place after you get saved, and it is used to let the world or others know that you have been converted; and now you are a follower of Christ. It is a testimonial to others that you have become a Christian. *Mk 1:5: And there went out unto him all the land of Judaea, and they of Jerusalem, and were all baptized of him in the river of Jordan, confessing their sins.*

In other words, you have to tell everyone of your conversion and be open about it. It is not a secret; God wants it to be public, letting others know of the experience you just had with your Savior.

In the next verse, we have the story of a doctor of the law of the Old Testament, supposedly very educated man of his time! He came to Jesus to inquire about salvation. Jesus then went right to the point. *John 3:3: Jesus answered and said unto him, Verily, verily, I say unto thee, Except a man be born again, he cannot see the kingdom of God.*

He is showing Nicodemus the steps he needs to take to become a Christian; born again is used here to describe what we did in the previous chapter or how to get saved. Then He goes to the next step. *John 3:5: Jesus answered, Verily, verily, I say unto thee, Except a man be born of water and of the Spirit, he cannot enter into the kingdom of God.*

This step born of water also refers to as the Baptism of Repentance by Paul here in *Acts 19:4: Then said Paul, John verily baptized with the baptism of repentance, saying unto the people, that they should believe on him which should come after him, that is, on Christ Jesus.*

We have now all three steps that I am covering in this book. Born again which is how to be saved, then to be baptized by water as a testimony to the people of our conversion, and last is born of the Spirit. This last one will be covered it in the final Step or chapter.

One thing we need to notice here is how essential Jesus made it and for us to know that without being born of water combine with confession and repentance as Paul says it above; and born of The Spirit. We cannot enter into His Kingdom.

As for this water baptism, we find a case where the person had no way or chance to be baptized, and yet Jesus gave him the authority to enter into His Kingdome from where he was, or just before he died *Luc.23:43 And Jesus said unto him, Verily I say unto thee, To day shalt thou be with me in paradise.*

This is in reference to one of the two thieves that were crucified with Jesus at Calvary. But also giving the idea that some can repent on their death bed. The Water Baptism, because it uses water, it has a relation in the Bible to cleanliness and being wash *Ps. 51:2 Wash me thoroughly from mine iniquity, and cleanse me from my sin. :7 Purge me with hyssop, and I shall be clean: wash me, and I shall be whiter than snow.*

On this verse 7, is a form of deeper cleansing with hyssop as a cleanser, similar to bleach we use today to make white garments whiter. In this case, David is talking about his desire to be as clean as possible.

This Baptism here is referred to as a doctrine *He. 6:2 Of the doctrine of baptisms, and of laying on of hands, and of resurrection of the dead, and of eternal judgment.*

Water Baptism then, either means or signifies the <u>following Items 1 to 8</u>!

#1   REPENTANCE: *Luc. 3:3: And he came into all the country about Jordan, preaching the baptism of repentance for the remission of sins; Acts. 19:4 Then said Paul, John verily baptized with the baptism of repentance, saying unto the people, that they should believe on him which should come after him, that is, on Christ Jesus.*

#2   CONFESSION: *Mat. 3:6 And were baptized of him in Jordan, confessing their sins.*

#3   WASH: *Acts. 22:16 And now why tarriest thou? arise, and be baptized, and wash away thy sins, calling on the name of the Lord.*

#4   CRUCIFIXION: *Rom. 6:6 Knowing this, that our old man is crucified with him, that the body of sin might be destroyed, that henceforth we should not serve sin.*

#5   DEATH: Rom. *6:4 Therefore we are buried with him by baptism into death: that like as Christ was raised up from the dead by the glory of the Father, even so we also should walk in newness of life.*

#6   BURIED: *Col. 2:12a Buried with him in baptism, wherein also ye are risen with him through the faith of the operation of God, who hath raised him from the dead.*

#7   RAISED: *Col. 2:12b Buried with him in baptism, wherein also ye are risen with him through the faith of the operation of God, who hath raised him from the dead.*

#8   RESURRECTION: *Rom. 6:4: Therefore we are buried with him by baptism into death: that like as Christ was raised up from the dead by the glory of the Father, even so we also should walk in newness of life. 5: For if we have been planted together in the likeness of his death, we shall be also in the likeness of his resurrection:*

Everything that is described above is primarily for our own enrichment of what the Scriptures are telling us, and how to proceed as we try to obey and fulfilled its requirements, and know that we are doing all of it the right way, and according to His will; and the way He has laid it for us to follow.

The Bible does not give us a specific timing for this event, other than it takes place after confession of our sins, or after getting saved. The idea here is to bring it out on the open, and to let others know that we are new creatures in Christ, and now we belong to Him. So there is a change of heart, and from now on, we will have a new life and the desire to tell others about it.

Because of what it signifies, this leaves out the idea of baptizing babies. There are churches that have supplemented the baptism of babies by dedicating them instead, and it should not be done until they grow-up to an age of understanding of their own. For the reason for this baptism of water.

Also leaves out the idea of sprinkling a person when baptizing, rather it be of submersion as it signifies washing, being buried, like a seed in the ground. Meaning, you need to die, so you can be raised from the dead, resurrected.

CHAPTER THREE

THE BAPTISM OF THE HOLY SPIRIT

PHASE 3

As we try to put the pieces together about this particular step of our salvation, we need to remember and keep in mind that it is on the spiritual side, and perhaps it is a little hard to comprehend. This is part of our connection with God that Adam and Eve lost when they sin. This was the part that caused them to be thrown off the garden.

As a result of that sin, the contract between them and God was terminated. The relationship between God and them got broken. It causes them to die spiritually, when Adam and Eve could not keep this one commandment. The scripture tells us that they die as a result of it. *Gen. 2:17 But of the tree of the knowledge of good and evil, thou shalt not eat of it: for in the day that thou eatest thereof thou shalt surely die.*

This Baptism of the Holy Spirit is one of the most debated and misunderstood subjects we find in the Scriptures when it comes to this step of our salvation. It has been for some time, the realm of many discussions and debatable theories on when and how it takes place.

And also because of the different groups trying to differ from each other, some refer to this step as sanctification, being this the wrong description of it, since the word sanctified means to be set apart or separated *Jude 1:1 Jude, the servant of Jesus Christ, and brother of James, to them that are sanctified by God the Father, and preserved in Jesus Christ, and called:*

In this next verse we see how this word is used *1 Cor 7:14 For the unbelieving husband is sanctified by the wife, and the unbelieving wife is sanctified by the husband: else were your children unclean; but now are they holy.*

Here we can see Paul using this word sanctified to describe a nonbeliever either a husband or wife that has indirect connection with Christ through a spouse that is a believer of Christ, but that person still remains an unbeliever, and this has nothing to do with the gift and Baptism of The Holy Spirit. Being this step the last that completes our salvation.

The Bible uses it in different places, referring to it, as the baptism of The Holy Spirit, like we have on this statement by John when he said in this next verse: *Mk 1:8 I indeed have baptized you with water: but he shall baptize you with the Holy Ghost.*

Meaning, Christ is the only one, who can baptize us with the Holy Spirit, in order to take care of the sin we are born with. Christ can perform this step, without any intervention or participation of our own. Meaning, you cannot repent of it, for possessing it, and you need to deal with it, take care of. But most importantly, this sin has to be removed from us. As Christians, we cannot live with this original sin within us. Eventually will drag us down. He made it clear that it cannot be in the presence of God. We are told in: *Mat.5:20 For I say unto you, That except your righteousness shall exceed the righteousness of the scribes and Pharisees, ye shall in no case enter into the kingdom of heaven. 18:3 And said, Verily I say unto you, Except ye be converted, and become as little children, ye shall not enter into the kingdom of heaven.*

Although we probably agree that this is a very essential ingredient to the completion of our salvation/conversion, and transformation of our lives to be completely surrendered to the serving of our Lord and Savior.

The Scriptures tells us that it is required, *John 3:5 Jesus answered, Verily, verily, I say unto thee, Except a man be born of water and of the Spirit, he cannot enter into the kingdom of God. Acts 2:4: And they were all filled with the Holy Ghost, and began to speak with other tongues, as the Spirit gave them utterance.*

If you remember that we discussed in the first chapter, about the two types of sins that we possess?

1) The first one is the one we are born with or inherit it from our ancestors, and it has been passed on to us from Adam and Eve.

2) The other one is the one we commit ourselves. This one is taken care of when we repent and confess our sins to Jesus/God and get baptized with water.

This step or the baptism of the Holy Spirit, as it has been mention above, will take care of that inherited sin, or should we say, God will remove the original sin out of our heart/lives altogether.

This is something that we cannot repent from, or we cannot be accountable for, as it comes from our forefathers.

This sin that has been pass all the way along to us. In other words we are born with it. Is one of those things that we can't live with, and be Christians at the same time. Because it will interfere with our Christian journey and eventually will bring us down or will take us back to where we got started from. Paul describes this in: *Rom. 7:20: Now if I do that I would not, it is no more I that do it, but sin that dwelleth in me.*

Somewhere in our life it has to be taken care of, or have to get rid of it, because it cannot enter heaven, and most importantly, we can't be Christians until sin it is completely out of our lives. As long this original sin dwells in us it will keep us from growing in grace. *1 Pt 2:2 As newborn babes, desire the sincere milk of the word, that ye may grow thereby.*

As Paul said it, it will continue to cause us to sin. As long as it remains in us.

This is one of the things that happens when a newborn comes into this world, that Satan takes residence in that person's heart (refer to as the mind, or the center of our being) when we step into this world or breathe air for the first time. The Bible tells us that by one-man sin enter into the world *Rom. 5:12 Wherefore, as by one man sin entered into the world, and death by sin; and so death passed upon all men, for that all have sinned:*

It tells us that we all are sinners, even when we have not committed any sin of our own. Do you know that little babies do get angry early in life? Where do you think that comes from? I think that this is an indication of the presence of the original sin in them.

Here is where The Holy Spirit comes in and removes that original sin that had possessed us since we were born. This possession that sin through Satan has taken over our life and lives within us. Therefore, God does the eviction of Satan from our hearts, through this step of the baptism of The Holy Spirit; removing the original sin from our hearts.

Jesus also said, all are born of the flash. Meaning, when we are born in the physical body, we are posses by sin, therefore, we must be born of The Spirit, in order to take care of that inherited original sin. *John 3:6 That which is born of the flesh is flesh; and that which is born of the Spirit is spirit.*

The sad part is that no one can do anything about it, Except God Himself. That is why He has provided the solution to this problem. It is a must Jesus told Nicodemus in: *John 3:7 Marvel not that I said unto thee, Ye must be born again.*

Telling him that he has to complete the necessary requirements in order to be born again, believe and repent, and to be baptized with water as a testimony of our conversion; then the gift of the Holy Spirit, *Lk. 11:13: If ye then, being evil, know how to give good gifts unto your children: how much more shall your heavenly Father give the Holy Spirit to them that ask him?*

God mention it that is a gift whenever one repents of their Sins. *Acts.2:38 Then Peter said unto them, Repent, and be baptized every one of you in the name of Jesus Christ for the remission of sins, and ye shall receive the gift of the Holy Ghost.*

Based on what we just read and about what Peter said; this is all that we need to do when pursuing "**the purpose of our life**."

It is needed to be in the proper relationship with God, and to be a candidate for heaven. But also to live our life to its fullness as God intended for our life to be, and be able to enjoy it to the max. That would be an impossible task to do, if the original sin remains within us.

You might say, "Who cares about heaven?" You would be Right because most people don't. That does not mean you don't need God's forgiveness, and you don't need to repent; The reality is we do! There are only two ways to go about it. The narrow door which will take you to heaven, *Mt 7:14 Because strait is the gate, and narrow is the way, which leadeth unto life, and few there be that find it. Or take the wide gate, which will lead you to perdition and eternal damnation. Mt 7:13 Enter ye in at the strait gate: for wide is the gate, and broad is the way, that leadeth to destruction, and many there be which go in thereat:*

Base on the two choices that we have, should we say: NOW IS OUR CALL, you pick; you choose which way you want your life to go.

This choice will determine where you will be when life is all over, and ultimately which place you will end up at.

Keeping in mind that there are only two ways to go about it! You either will go **Up** or **Down**, you are either **In** or **Out**, you'll pick **Good** or **Evil**. Your choice and no one can make it for you. You will not be forced to go either way. God has given us that privilege to choose what we want. Even though when we have this privilege, Jesus remains faithful to us and keeps knocking at our door *Rv 3:20 Behold, I stand at the door, and knock: if any man hear my voice, and open the door, I will come in to him, and will sup with him, and he with me.*

You have the option not to answer the call, and keep your door closed. I remember hearing about this person that went as far as to ask Jesus not to bother him anymore and leave him alone. Jesus granted his wish and stop calling him. Then one day this person realized that God really left him alone. At that point he knew that now it was up to him to take the next step, and go to God and ask Him for an apology and forgiveness for his sins and to start his recovery process. Even after all the mess this guy made, God was there faithfully waiting for him and ready to forgive him.

Being a dangers position to be in or to take, it is not guaranty that we can ever do the same. Death can call on us at any instant, even before we can go to God; and we might not have the same opportunity to repent.

Continuing with our subject, and as I mention above, it is a gift, after we confess our sins. Being this a special gift for those who repent of their sins; thus completing their salvation. God knows this, and that is why He has prepared a plan of salvation for all mankind. *Mat. 25: 34: Then shall the King say unto them on his right hand, Come, ye blessed of my Father, inherit the kingdom prepared for you from the foundation of the world:*

It is not necessary for us to know how God does it. Being that it is instantaneous, a supernatural work of God. In other words God does not have to serve the old tenant (Satan) living in our heart/mind an eviction notice, after you decide to go on God's way, He just comes in and puts him out, based on *Mathew: 3:11 I indeed baptize you with water unto repentance: but he that cometh after me is mightier than I, whose shoes I am not worthy to bear: he shall baptize you with the Holy Ghost, and with fire:*

He uses fire to burn everything that Satan had accumulated in us, thus performing a thorough cleaning process and closes the door. No lock though! Unfortunately! Satan can still come back in and reclaim us, if we let him back again, by us continuing with our old ways, or we persist to live the same way as before we repented, in sin, and run a very high risk of losing our salvation and becoming our old selves again. *1 Thes. 3:8 For now we live, if ye stand fast in the Lord.*

Meaning that it takes an effort of ours to stand fast in order to maintain that relationship with God, or we will fall *1 Cor. 10:12 Wherefore let him that thinketh he standeth take heed lest he fall.*

This is a process that takes place in ourselves to make sure we continue to nourish our spiritual growth, by constantly maintaining it. With Gods help. *1 Co. 10:23 All things are lawful for me, but all things are not expedient: all things are lawful for me, but all things edify not.*

In other words, be on your guard at all times; and learn of His ways.

There are too many people who go through the motions of getting saved and think that they can continue with their old ways: meaning that they never repented of their sin. If they really repented of their sin but continue to practice it, then they run the risk of becoming a backslider and find themselves back in sin again, back to where they got started from. If this is not taken care of, and really mean business, you run the risk of losing it all. One of the things to keep in mind is that you cannot fool God. But if you are for real, but fail to complete this last step in your conversion, you will run the risk of falling by not receiving this Baptism of The Holy Spirit. The reason being is that you still have and are living with the original sin within you. *Heb. 12:15 Looking diligently lest any man fail of the grace of God; lest any root of bitterness springing up trouble you, and thereby many be defiled.*

What we read in this verse is that, if you continue to live with the original sin in your heart/mind, eventually will take you down if you let it live, and it continues to reside within your heart/mind.

Remember, this is the sin that will make you and causes you to commit your own sins. Therefore, it must be revoked/removed out of yourself (heart/mind), and that is what the baptism of The Holy Spirit does. There must not be any sin left in you after your conversion, for too long. Here is where others come in and should help us to complete all the steps necessary. That is why it has never been suggested for us to do it all on our own, we need the help of others and God Himself to accomplish all of it. And remember that this step it is not optional, it's a must, in order for both sins to be removed from us or our life; the original sin and the sin of omission(ours).

Another way to describe it is: When we believe and are baptized with water of repentance, is like cutting down a tree, the tree is the product of the root which is the original sin. By leaving the roots and trunk in the ground, in time will spring up a new branch through the trunk and it will become a little tree or trees. It is hard to know how many trees can be produce from, and start to grow from that old trunk.

It will bring perhaps more trouble than ever before. But also it will take us back to the old ways or should we say! It will cause us to sin again. And most of the time it is worse than ever before. *Mat. 12:45 Then goeth he, and taketh with himself seven other spirits more wicked than himself, and they enter in and dwell there: and the last state of that man is worse than the first. Even so shall it be also unto this wicked generation.*

This is what the Holy Spirit does. He removes the old trunk and roots all together, completely out, making you clean of all sin.

Actually, letting us start from scratch, and even then, we still are vulnerable to a fall. Meaning that Satan will try with all his power to regain his possession, which he just lost to Christ when we became saved and completed all the steps that Jesus require for our salvation. The one good thing is that he (Satan) will be fighting us from the outside; instead of the inside. Throwing and enticing you with anything he knows you are weak at. And believe it; he knows you better than you know yourself. But, fighting him when he is on the outside puts us at a better advantage, and a better chance to resist him and be successful at it. *Jms 4:7 Submit yourselves therefore to God. Resist the devil, and he will flee from you.*

It is much easier when we know that this fight is not from within. Way different than when you have to fight him when he is still in us, which usually is at our disadvantage; or should we say before the Baptism of The Holy Spirit.

This is one way to know if you have been giving and you have received this gift of the Spirit. Having Satan in our selves makes it easier to commit sin, verses him being on the outside.

1 Pt. 5:9: Whom resist steadfast in the faith, knowing that the same afflictions are accomplished in your brethren that are in the world.

When this phase takes place? We have two (2) Different examples that are very clear in The Bible. You can receive this gift when you repent, and other times after your repentance, not necessary at the same time. Next!

EXAMINING THE TWO EXAMPLES!

#1 First example is described in the next verses *Acts 10:44 While Peter yet spake these words, the Holy Ghost fell on all them which heard the word.*

45: *And they of the circumcision which believed were astonished, as many as came with Peter, because that on the Gentiles also was poured out the gift of the Holy Ghost. 46: For they heard them speak with tongues, and magnify God. Then answered Peter,*

47: *Can any man forbid water, that these should not be baptized, which have received the Holy Ghost as well as we?*

In this case they repented as Peter was talking to them and receive The Holy Spirit at the same time. Then Peter suggested that they should be baptized with water to give testimony of their conversion, thus completing the requirements set by Jesus Christ.

#2- The second one is when Peter and John were sent to Samaria *Acts. 8:14 Now when the apostles which were at Jerusalem heard that Samaria had received the word of God, they sent unto them Peter and John: Who, when they were come down, prayed for them, that they might receive the Holy Ghost:*

15: *(For as yet he was fallen upon none of them: only they were baptized in the name of the Lord Jesus.)*

16: *Then laid they their hands on them, and they received the Holy Ghost.*

Here we have it, and it is very clear that time has transpired and yet they were able to receive this gift of The Holy Spirit, after and on a different time of their repentance and conversion; Being this baptism of the Holy Spirit one of the important requirements to complete their Salvation.

Next! Tongues! A much-debated subject!

God used tongues or languages to include everyone present, showing all peoples what He was giving to them, as He gave this gift of The Holy Spirit as part of their salvation, when they gave their life to Christ.

We need to take into an account, that speaking in tongues did not occur in Samaria. My speculation is that there were only locals. There were no outsiders from other towns with different languages, who could have been included in their testimonial of this very important event when they receive the gift of The Holy Spirit.

We read in the next passage: *Acts. 2:7 And they were all amazed and marvelled, saying one to another, Behold, are not all these which speak Galileans?*

8: *And how hear we every man in our own tongue, wherein we were born?*

9: *Parthians, and Medes, and Elamites, and the dwellers in Mesopotamia, and in Judaea, and Cappadocia, in Pontus, and Asia,*

10: *Phrygia, and Pamphylia, in Egypt, and in the parts of Libya about Cyrene, and strangers of Rome, Jews and proselytes,*

11: *Cretes and Arabians, we do hear them speak in our tongues the wonderful works of God.*

It tells us that there were different peoples, from diverse places with different languages, real languages, that people use to communicate with each other; not like the tongue that some groups have introduced as evidence when they receive The Holy Spirit as they like us to believe. They call it an angelic tongue, something that if there was such a thing, (angelic language that humans can practice) is not for humans to use. It is obvious that angelic beings have a type of communication system among themselves but it's different from ours, as humans with physical bodies.

My reason for dismissing this idea of angelic language that some Christians claim to possess is because this form of communication between humans or other creatures like animals that have a body being of a physical form.

We make an actual noise created by muscles found in the human or animal body (flesh if you will); that muscle called vocal cord, something that an angelic being does not possess. They do not have physical body with vocal cord like humans or animals do.

The scripture tells us that when the first Christians spoke in other tongues, it is referring to it as: A real language or form of human communication with words produce by vocal sound, like Hebrew, Greek, Aramaic, or maybe we can include English, Spanish, French and Italian.

As we can see here, God wanted to show the people and also He wanted for everyone to hear on their own language, how they can partake of the Gospel or the plan of salvation that He has made available for us all. We can see here that not one person was left out. They all were included when they witness this historical event. As a result of it, 3 thousand people were saved that day. *Acts 2:41 Then they that gladly received his word were baptized: and the same day there were added unto them about three thousand souls.*

The point is that we can receive this gift of The Holy Spirit. In some cases, at the same time as you repent of your sins or can be after you confessed your sins and even after your baptism of water. But never has been before your confession. All depended at that time on what the circumstances were and the geographical place at the time of their conversion, when this event took place. For us today is much different than at the beginning of the Christian church. Christianity has grown and have spread around the world and we see that the evidence of speaking in tongues (language) has diminish with time as we do not have that integration that occurs at the time of the Apostles. As a rule, we go to churches that speak our language or we understand theirs; but Christ is also much more known today versus from the time of the beginning of the Christian Church.

Looking at the requirements, as Jesus described them above, we need to follow them in their proper order to insure our salvation and start our walk as new born in Christ. We achieve **the path of life's purpose**, by following it to the foot of the letter. Then we can walk to the end of our existence with this life that we have been entrusted with and it has been given to us freely. Making sure that we have follow His rules.

So how do we take care of this one step? As we just noted above, you can either get it when we repent or can be after. On either case you will know when you received it. One of the ways to know that you have it is that when you are born again as Jesus said. Is that you will have a sense of internal peace within yourself which will change your internal feelings towards others and life in general. It is an experience that is hard to explain and sometimes there are no words to described it. But one thing is for sure! It does affect your feelings in an outward manor that others will know that something has happened to you. You will have a new life with in you and it will spring out of you. One of the things is that you will want to share it with others as well, depending on the character that you possess. You might not be as open as others, but it will be noticeable in you. Your internal cleanliness will reflect outwardly.

Your immediate family and friends will know that something has happened to you. And that is something you will want to share and talk about. Plus, you will want people to know that you are a Christian now. Your talk will change almost automatically as well as the way you conduct yourself with others and many times will include the way you dress. No mistake about it it's something real and it does change people; and this is something you will not regret, but instead you will be glad you have taken this very important step in your life.

Now, when people know that you are a Christian, it is surprisingly very satisfying, especially when you are approached by someone and ask you if you are a Christian. Somehow, they will notice something about you that you look different. I have asked them! How do you know I am a Christian? Their answer was, you just look like one and act like one. And also, I have been asked if I was a preacher! That, for me, was a bigger surprise. But more than that was when they knew that I was a Christian; they watched my language. I remember when I was told by this one person that I can't say or use bad words! Christians don't talk that way! He told me. And never forgot it.

In another conversation with the same person, he though I have said a bad word, which I had not, but he thought I had said it. I told him that those words are no longer in my vocabulary. Somehow, he knew that Christians should not use bad language.

Taking all of this into consideration, has given me a bigger responsibility on how I look and conduct myself when I'm around others. But most importantly is on how I'm reflecting Christ to people. I do want to be able to lead others to Christ, and have the satisfaction in myself of being able to help them into this process, bringing them to know Christ on a personal way or relationship.

It is an experience of a lifetime, when you know that there is nothing wrong within yourself, and know that now we are capable to live this life to the fullest.

You can't buy it or try to substitute it with anything else, not even with expensive and costly possessions, or psychological treatments.

It is free, we just need to follow Christ's requirements Described above. Remember that the last ingredient we just discussed. God is the only one who can take care of it.

What I am trying to say is, that salvation is a two (2) part Procedure. 1-The first part is ours. We are required to repent and confess our sins. 2- The second part is Gods only. He is the one who takes care of the original sin. We just have to do ours, and He will do the rest; or with the prayers of others as we read it above to get it done.

CHAPTER FOUR

||||||||||||||||||||||||||||||||||||||||

ANALYZING A CLOSER LOOK TO WHAT WE JUST ACCOMPLISHED!

At this point, we have taken all the steps and have fulfill all the requirements that God has laid in for us in order to be saved. But most important is **<u>Finding the way to our life's purpose</u>** according to God.

1-) We have seen, heard it, or we have read The Bible, or any other related literature on how to be saved, and came to the conclusion that we are sinners and have the need to repent and confess our sins and receive the forgiveness of God.

2-) But also made the decision to becoming a Christian, and to be a follower of Christ; or we could have chosen to go the opposite way. That is by picking the Broader way we read in the previous chapter, described to be one of the choices.

3-) We also understand that as part of the requirement, we need to be baptized by water, as part of our testimony of our conversion, to show the world and let others know that we have become Christians.

4-) Last, we receive the gift of The Holy Spirit when we repented or maybe in a separate occasion, afterwards, which as part of our conversion, by being prayed for. And by the laying of hands, we receive The Holy Spirit. This completes our conversion from our state of life as we know it, to now a new way of Godly life in Christ.

ONE VERY IMPORTANT OBSERVATION!

Until you complete those steps described above, you cannot go forward with your Christian growth. You have to be completely saved, not partially save, before you can start and continue to grow spiritually. Your life will be at a standing still state if you do not allow Him to perform all of His requirements in ourselves by removing the two types of sin.

A better description of how this works is by comparing it to the likeness of our education, as you work towards your school diploma. You cannot graduate from high school, if you miss one of the grades. As a rule, you have to complete all your assignments required by the school system, before they can give you the diploma that proves the completion of all your necessary assignments. If along the way you fail to pass any of those grades, most likely they will have you retake it until you complete it you cannot go to the next one. But not until then you can pick where to go next as far as your education is concern. You will not be able to go to or start college, if you have not completed your High School.

It is pretty much the same way in this case. You have to follow the proper channels and fulfill all the requirements, otherwise you cannot continue to go to the next step. By not completing them, you will not be able to grow spiritually. It will handicap you even to the place that you might lose all of it. Paul tells us that there is a growth we need to follow *1 Cor3:2 I have fed you with milk, and not with meat: for hitherto ye were not able to bear it, neither yet now are ye able. 1 Co. 13:11: When I was a child, I spake as a child, I understood as a child, I thought as a child: but when I became a man, I put away childish things.*

Meaning that there is a period of growth when you start your new life with Christ. Others will try to bypass it when they try to cheat their way out of it. *Jn 10:1 Verily, verily, I say unto you, He that entereth not by the door into the sheepfold, but climbeth up some other way, the same is a thief and a robber.*

In this case we can say that we have to, and need to go through the proper channels. And most importantly, have to note that, as a Christian, it will keep us from developing to what God wants you to be. Worst of all, it can keep us from entering into heaven. By now we know that sin is not allow in heaven, furthermore it will also detour us of the way and direction you could go in your life. In some cases, it will rob us from the privilege or privileges of being used by God. We can end-up perhaps missing it all together. And as a Christian sometimes we will wonder why we can't seem to go any farther with your Christian life. Surprisingly there are too many of those out there which in term is very sad. And as far as some of those gifts are concerned he says. *1 Cor 12:4 Now there are diversities of gifts, but the same Spirit. 5: And there are differences of administrations, but the same Lord. 6: And there are diversities of operations, but it is the same God which worketh all in all. 7: But the manifestation of the Spirit is given to every man to profit withal.*

Meaning, some of those gifts will not be properly executed by you if you do not qualify to receive them. Ultimately, what I have seen is: People that don't qualify are trying to do God's work without His approval and blessings. They not only have missed the point but also will end up missing everything. The sad part is that too many people are playing church and ultimately playing with their own life, in the name of Jesus. *Mt. 7:22 Many will say to me in that day, Lord, Lord, have we not prophesied in thy name? and in thy name have cast out devils? and in thy name done many wonderful works?*
23: And then will I profess unto them, I never knew you: depart from me, ye that work iniquity.

So, on the long run it does pay to follow God's ways and not ours.

Next: <u>Let's look at what happened and what an impact this procedure will do in our life.</u>

By pointing some of the things that do happen when someone gets saved.

1-) You will become a new creature in Christ. Therefore you will be a new person to your family, and based on your gender, you will either be a new son or daughter, brother or sister, husband or wife, father or mother, and even a new neighbor, and in general a new person to all. It will be a new you. But the most important of all is that your relationship with God is now restored to its original state, and you become again either sons or daughters of the most High, Jesus said it in: *John 1:12: But as many as received him, to them gave he power to become the sons of God, even to them that believe on his name:*

 (Note: Not until our life is restored; we are nothing but God's creation). I had conversations with some people telling me that they consider themselves to be either sons or daughters of God, thinking that all men kind automatically we are the sons and daughters. Unfortunately, we are not until we become Christians. When sin came into mankind, we lost that title. And it is not restored until you repent and complete all the steps mention above in order to restore that title as we read it above in John 1:12.

2-) It will change your life when you are forgiven by God for your sins. But not only that; immediately you will have a new look at people around you as well as to life in general. It is a wonderful filing when you know that you have been forgiven of your sins, even when you might think that you don't have any. *Rom 3:23 For all have sinned, and come short of the glory of God.*

 We all are born in sin and that alone requires the forgiveness of God and the baptism or gift of The Holy Spirit in order to eradicate the original sin that came within us when we are born into this world.

3-) After all of this, here are some of the things you either have read or will read in the scriptures (Bible), they will start to make sense to you. This is a privilege given only to Christians or in this case, to God's new members of His family *1 Cor 2:14 But the natural man receiveth not the things of the Spirit of God: for they are foolishness unto him: neither can he know them, because they are spiritually discerned.*

In this case we are now in a restored state of mind, spiritually, our spiritual eyes are open as well as our communication with the Creator. You are now in the position to make your own petitions. In other words, now you can talk to or pray directly to Him, and continue to have that relationship with Him, that up to this point have been lost; but also you will receive all the blessings He has in store for us as his Children. *Heb 11:6 But without faith it is impossible to please him: for he that cometh to God must believe that he is, and that he is a rewarder of them that diligently seek him.*

Until then, anything you do and say to God will not have any response from Him, unless you come to Him with a heart or state of repentance. *1 Pet. 3:12: For the eyes of the Lord are over the righteous, and his ears are open unto their prayers: but the face of the Lord is against them that do evil.*

Sometimes we might even receive instruction directly from God. Referring to that small voice that comes either from God, but also, it can be from the wrong source or spirit. Now, This being a very sensitive subject! There are many people who claim to have receive instructions from God, but fail to support them with God's written word. If you receive an instruction directly from God, it has to be in an agreement, and you should be able to back it up with Gods already written word, The Bible. Then you can proceed with the instruction/s given to you. But if it is not in accordance or in sink with the Bible and you cannot support it with His written scriptures then it's most likely that is not to be from God Himself. *1Jn 4:1 Beloved, believe not every spirit, but try the spirits whether they are of God: because many false prophets are gone out into the world.*

He will never give you or say anything to you that contradicts His own written Word (The Bible).

I have come across people who told me that God have given them instruction to say or do certain things, but it was obvious that they were not Bible base. Immediately I was able to notes that it had to be from the wrong source. In cases like this you have to know your Bible pretty good, in order to make a comparison to what you just herd and what appears to be from God. It pays having read the Bible to be prepared for the tricks of the enemy (the devil). "For the record: one of the gifts of The Spirit is discerning spirits."
1 Cor 12:10 To another the working of miracles; to another prophecy; to another discerning of spirits; to another divers kinds of tongues; to another the interpretation of tongues:
One of the things is that you have to use your own common scents, and not go overboard with God telling you and giving you personal instructions. For example: You will start by asking God what color shoes you should ware, He might sometimes, but not on every time you put a pair of shoes.

You might depend on that instead of reading your Bible. There will be times when we need to ask God for directions as it is necessary, but we also need to be prepared for the answer, as it might come from the wrong source. This is another way, where having some knowledge of the scriptures becomes handy. At this point we need to focus more on how to grow spiritually, by reading His Word and learn more of what He has to say to us through the Bible *2 Tm 3:15 And that from a child thou hast known the holy scriptures, which are able to make thee wise unto salvation through faith which is in Christ Jesus.*

Obviously, He will guide us, and we will know what steps to take in life. He will do just that, and will guide us in the right path, and to do the right things, and will help us become the person we ought to be, and wants us to be, by keeping it all synchronized. Also, being able to discern some of those things can be limited, based on how much knowledge of the Bible we possess. *Rom 15:14 And I myself also am persuaded of you, my brethren, that ye also are full of goodness, filled with all knowledge, able also to admonish one another.*

Don't get me wrong, but there are times when God will direct us to what route to take, but we need to be prepared to obey Him; and make sure to discern where that help comes from. If He is to call anyone, He will not leave you alone. *Jn 14:18 I will not leave you comfortless: I will come to you.*

I can safely say that there are a lot of people out there who can say that He has never let us down. One good thing about all of this is that many times, based on your knowledge of His word, He will let you know when you are about to do something wrong. Then it will be up to you to either obey or disobey that voice that comes to your mind with the warning.

From now on, it will be up to us to follow God's word (The Bible) and to continue to read it and studied it, but also to put it into practice in order to make us successful Christians and make Him worthy of our praise. *Jms 1:22 But be ye doers of the word, and not hearers only, deceiving your own selves.*

Don't forget that from this point on, we will not only be representing but also reflecting Him; in whatever we do and say. Whether you like it or not, people will be watching you to see how you will handle yourself and will be watching your development now that you became a Christian. They would want to see if you are for real and how long will you last.

The point here is that with your life, you will have the ability to become a good Christian, but also you will have the desire to help others to grow as well; also help someone to come to Christ with your example. And with your actions, you can encourage someone to come to Christ and help them to grow as well. At the same time, you can also discourage someone from ever coming to Christ.

Nevertheless, whatever happens from now on, it will be a much better way of life you can ever experience in comparison with the one you were living, without Christ. You will never come to the place where you can say that you regret that time when you surrendered your life to Christ.

In some cases, it is profitable to practice God's laws even when you are not a Christian. Keep in mind that in the beginning, it will take an effort on your part to make it all happen. It is not an automatic deal. It will take dedication and devotion on your part to achieve this goal *Mt 11:12 And from the days of John the Baptist until now the kingdom of heaven suffereth violence, and the violent take it by force.*

Meaning that salvation is up for grab, and it takes a little bit of calculated desire and ambition on the part of the pursuer. *Mt 7:14 Because strait is the gate, and narrow is the way, which leadeth unto life, and few there be that find it.*

Even though you can come across this great salvation, it will take your complete admiration and grate desire from yourself to obtain it, also dedication and full devotion to maintain it. *Mt 5:20 For I say unto you, That except your righteousness shall exceed the righteousness of the scribes and Pharisees, ye shall in no case enter into the kingdom of heaven.*

Here on this passage, we are to exceed the righteousness of theirs which got distorted by them adding rules of their own. Instead of helping themselves they got side tract from the real intentions that God had for them. So whatever the scribes and Pharisees were doing, it fails them completely, or the results thereof were very poor and unacceptable.

As for our endeavors, all will be worthy at the end of our journey. *1Cor 2:9 But as it is written, Eye hath not seen, nor ear heard, neither have entered into the heart of man, the things which God hath prepared for them that love him.*

Based on what we have read so far, and by using our Imagination, it is obvious that God have and still is doing His part. He is doing all He can to bring as many people as possible to Himself. To describe it in our own words as to say: It will be in style, with the best sophistication and appearance you can ever imagine, and to top it all on, will be the most glamorous home coming you can ever fathom. We get an idea from the next story of the prodigal son. *Luc 15:21: And the son said unto him, Father, I have sinned against heaven, and in thy sight, and am no more worthy to be called thy son.*

22: But the father said to his servants, Bring forth the best robe, and put it on him; and put a ring on his hand, and shoes on his feet:

23: And bring hither the fatted calf, and kill it; and let us eat, and be merry:

24: For this my son was dead, and is alive again; he was lost, and is found. And they began to be merry.

25: Now his elder son was in the field: and as he came and drew nigh to the house, he heard music and dancing.

Talking about throwing a party, you might think that we know how to do such a thing! You could not even start to comprehend the glamour and sophistication involve in it. And who is the one giving this party? No other than the creator of everything, the Universe. That is a mind boggling.

Keep in mind that there are a lot of people who do not want to be there! Their option is to go on to the opposite direction. And where would that take them? I think that by now, you have a pretty good Idea to where that is.

Let us be the one who choose this narrow road, and to take a hold on it, and grab it as Mt. 11:12 says it above, and keep it until someday when we all are called and will cross to the other side. Will be looking forward to meeting you there; on that great supper of the Lamb. *Rv 19:9 And he saith unto me, Write, Blessed are they which are called unto the marriage supper of the Lamb. And he saith unto me, These are the true sayings of God.*

For our convenience I have included all the scriptures I referred to, from the King James Version of the Bible. Use all this information as a point of reference, whenever you decide to read it or to review it.

Once you have experience all the steps described above, there will be certain amount of responsibility on your part, to grow spiritually with God Himself at your side. And continue to maintain that connection and relationship with God/Jesus. Go all the way, until you are called into the next life. In the meantime you will need the support from other Christians, or visa versa, by also giving them your support. This is where Church comes into place, you will need to be part of one, and assist it on a regular basis. *Heb 10:25 Not forsaking the assembling of ourselves together, as the manner of some is; but exhorting one another: and so much the more, as ye see the day approaching. 1 Thes 5:11 Wherefore comfort yourselves together, and edify one another, even as also ye do.*

Being this a crucial part, you will grow cold, and will lose it all, if you are not diligent on all you do, and all you have accomplish. Up to this point, can be lost, if you decided to give yourself some slack. Something you can't afford to do; your own life depends on it. But if you decided to throw it away, you need to realize, that is not only your life you be throwing away, but perhaps the life of others as well. With your example, and the way you will represent Christ. Your life not only will have an impact but also will be affecting the life of others.

<u>This story is of someone whom I helped to come to Christ.</u>

It all got started one evening when my wife and I were holding an evening Church service. It happened to be across the street from this person's house. That evening I was delivering the message when he between two of his sisters who brought him and help him to kneel by the altar. To my surprise he was a very drunk man; he could not stand on his own. Naturally we stop what we were doing, and I came down to great them. Then I proceeded to ask him if he was ready to give his life to Christ and become a Christian and he said yes! He also proceeded to tell me that he was very tired of his kind of life (alcoholic) that he was living. So we knelt at the altar with me next to him and with some of the others in the service and told him to ask God for forgiveness of his sins, then we all pray with him no more than 5 minutes. When we finish praying, he stood up and to my surprise he got up on his own sober able to stand by himself. Then, I proceeded to shake his hand and welcome him to the Christian family. I also told him to start coming to Church on a regular bases and that I would help him with his Christian growth. He became regular to our services on two different churches we had and he was doing very well that when his wife saw what was happening she also got saved. Then I had to come to the States supposedly for one year; but I got stuck here and never went back.

Right after this guy's conversion, I try to get my father to give his life to Christ as well. Being that he had a similar problem. His response to me was: Talking about the guy he heard about becoming a Christian. My father made me a promise when he said to me; if this guy (the one that came drunk) would to remain as Christian? he also would give his life to Christ, and he would repent of his sins and would become a Christian as well. He said it in a tone of voice like he knew that this (the drunk guy)was not going to stand his ground, stay as Christian. Sad to say! But this guy never did. He went back to drinking and he die not to long after. He was pretty good for a while or until I left. Meaning that for some new Christians, it takes a lot more nourishment to develop, or until they can stand on their own two feet and be able to continue to grow in Christ. The sad part is that I never told this guy about my father.

At that time, I didn't think that it was the time or the place to put him on the spot; and tell him what was at stake if he did not remain as Christian himself. Maybe that would have forced him to remain as Christian, knowing that my dad's life also depended on him by remaining as a Christian.

Maybe I should have, but at that time I did not see it that way. Sad to say it but this guy never knew it and he went back to drinking and lost the battle. Both die as result of their alcoholism.

Now looking back, it seems like I should have interfered, forcing him to stay as Christian. But while I was there all seems to be going well and I never figure that God would have other plans for me.

What I'm trying to say here is that my desires and prayers are that you will be a successful Christian; "if you become one." With one thing in mind, just focus on Christ and heaven. Get a tight hold on salvation, keep your eyes on Jesus Christ our Savior and not on people; people will let you down but Christ never will.

There is a scripture that probably you heard about

Lk. 12:29 And seek not ye what ye shall eat, or what ye shall drink, neither be ye of doubtful mind. 30: For all these things do the nations of the world seek after: and your Father knoweth that ye have need of these things. 31: But rather seek ye the kingdom of God; and all these things shall be added unto you.

This is one of the passages where Christ is trying to have us understand how much He cares for us if we can just learn to trust Him. It says here that He will add all of those things; if we just seek Him first. And what are all of those things? Not diminishing anything; it means all and everything we need to sustain us in life. I can testify to that! He has taken care of me and my family as well. Sometimes perhaps more then we deserve even to the place where I have been surprised when The Lord does His part if I just do mine. And believe me He does His very well.

All I have to do is follow Him and do my part; and He will take care of the rest. Also I have seen it happened in other Christians as well. There is nothing better than to be in the center of God's will. It is very rewarding when you know everything is well between you and your creator.

In different occasions I found myself to be in tuff situations where if it wasn't because of Gods help; I would have ended on the wrong path by proceeding on my own. I learn that as long as keep His commandments, and I do my part He will do His. Let's do our best and be the best representatives Christ can ever have.

The End

APPENDIX

Heart/Mind tempering with: Description in Pg. 30 2nd Paragraph. to 24 2nd Paragraph.

Guidelines before start: Start at Pg. 34

Our response to His Call: Pg. 36

Excuses for rejecting the Gospel: Pg. 37 First Paragraph.

The effects of cigarettes: Pg. 37 last Paragraph.

Who can be saved: Pg. 39 middle of Pg.

What is salvation: Pg. 40 2rd Paragraph and most of Pg. 41-42

Salvation, what is it for: Pg. 42 #2

Salvation, do we need it: Pg. 43 #3 second Paragraph.

Ingredients needed for salvation: Pg. 45 to 49,

Baptism of water: Described in the second Chapter beginning on Pg. 50

Baptism of The Holy Spirit: Described in chapter 3 Pg. 54

Two ways to receive the Holy Spirit: Pg. 62-63 Second Paragraph

www.ingramcontent.com/pod-product-compliance
Lightning Source LLC
Chambersburg PA
CBHW031326060726
47590CB00003B/1340